Old Cookery Books and Ancient Cuisine

William Carew Hazlitt

Contents

OLD COOKERY BOOKS AND ANCIENT CUISINE

BY

William Carew Hazlitt

INTRODUCTORY

Man has been distinguished from other animals in various ways; but perhaps there is no particular in which he exhibits so marked a difference from the rest of creation--not even in the prehensile faculty resident in his hand--as in the objection to raw food, meat, and vegetables. He approximates to his inferior contemporaries only in the matter of fruit, salads, and oysters, not to mention wild-duck. He entertains no sympathy with the cannibal, who judges the flavour of his enemy improved by temporary commitment to a subterranean larder; yet, to be sure, he keeps his grouse and his venison till it approaches the condition of spoon-meat.

It naturally ensues, from the absence or scantiness of explicit or systematic information connected with the opening stages of such inquiries as the present, that the student is compelled to draw his own inferences from indirect or unwitting allusion; but so long as conjecture and hypothesis are not too freely indulged, this class of evidence is, as a rule, tolerably trustworthy, and is, moreover, open to verification.

When we pass from an examination of the state of the question as regarded Cookery in very early times among us, before an even more valuable art--that of Printing--was discovered, we shall find ourselves face to face with a rich and long chronological series of books on the Mystery, the titles and fore-fronts of which are often not without a kind of fragrance and *gout*.

As the space allotted to me is limited, and as the sketch left by Warner of the convivial habits and household arrangements of the Saxons or Normans in this island, as well as of the monastic institutions, is more copious than any which I could offer, it may be best to refer simply to his elaborate preface. But it may be pointed out generally that the establishment of the Norman sway not only purged of some of their Anglo-Danish barbarism the tables of the nobility and the higher classes, but did much to spread among the poor a thriftier manipulation of the articles of food by a resort to broths, messes, and hot-pots. In the poorer districts, in Normandy as well as in Brittany, Duke William would probably find very little alteration in the mode of preparing victuals from that which was in use in his day, eight hundred years ago, if (like another Arthur) he should return among his ancient compatriots; but in his adopted country he would see that there had been a considerable revolt from the common saucepan--not to add from the pseudo-Arthurian bag-pudding; and that the English artisan, if he could get a rump-steak or a leg of mutton once a week, was content to starve on the other six days.

Those who desire to be more amply informed of the domestic economy of the ancient court, and to study the ***minutiae***, into which I am precluded from entering, can easily gratify themselves in the pages of "The Ordinances and Regulations for the Government of the Royal Household," 1790; "The Northumberland Household Book;" and the various printed volumes of "Privy Purse Expenses" of royal and great personages, including "The Household Roll of Bishop Swinfield (1289-90)."

The late Mr. Green, in his "History of the English People" (1880-3, 4 vols. 8vo), does not seem to have concerned himself about the kitchens or gardens of the nation which he undertook to describe. Yet, what conspicuous elements these have been in our social and domestic progress, and what civilising factors!

To a proper and accurate appreciation of the cookery of ancient times among ourselves, a knowledge of its condition in other more or less neighbouring countries, and of the surrounding influences and conditions which marked the dawn of the art in England, and its slow transition to a luxurious excess, would be in strictness necessary; but I am tempted to refer the reader to an admirable series of papers which appeared on this subject in Barker's "Domestic Architecture," and were collected in 1861, under the title of "Our English Home: its Early History and Progress." In this little volume the author, who does not give his name, has drawn together in a succinct compass the collateral information which will help to render the following pages more luminous and interesting. An essay might be written on the appointments of the table only, their introduction, development, and multiplication.

The history and antiquities of the Culinary Art among the Greeks are handled with his usual care and skill by M.J.A. St. John in his "Manners and Customs of

Ancient Greece," 1842; and in the ***Biblia*** or Hebrew Scriptures we get an indirect insight into the method of cooking from the forms of sacrifice.

The earliest legend which remains to us of Hellenic gastronomy is associated with cannibalism. It is the story of Pelops--an episode almost pre-Homeric, where a certain rudimentary knowledge of dressing flesh, and even of disguising its real nature, is implied in the tale, as it descends to us; and the next in order of times is perhaps the familiar passage in the ***Odyssey***, recounting the adventures of Odysseus and his companions in the cave of Polyphemus. Here, again, we are introduced to a rude society of cave-dwellers, who eat human flesh, if not as an habitual diet, yet not only without reluctance, but with relish and enjoyment.

The ***Phagetica*** of Ennius, of which fragments remain, seems to be the most ancient treatise of the kind in Roman literature. It is supposed to relate an account of edible fishes; but in a complete state the work may very well have amounted to a general Manual on the subject. In relation even to Homer, the ***Phagetica*** is comparatively modern, following the ***Odyssey*** at a distance of some six centuries; and in the interval it is extremely likely that anthropophagy had become rarer among the Greeks, and that if they still continued to be cooking animals, they were relinquishing the practice of cooking one another.

Mr. Ferguson, again, has built on Athenaeus and other authorities a highly valuable paper on "The Formation of the Palate," and the late Mr. Coote, in the forty-first volume of "Archaeologia," has a second on the "Cuisine Bourgeoise" of ancient Rome. These two essays, with the "Fairfax Inventories" communicated to the forty-eighth volume of the "Archaeologia" by Mr. Peacock, cover much of the ground which had been scarcely traversed before by any scientific English inquirer. The importance of an insight into the culinary economy of the Romans lies in the obligations under which the more western nations of Europe are to it for nearly all that they at first knew upon the subject. The Romans, on their part, were borrowers in this, as in other, sciences from Greece, where the arts of cookery and medicine were associated, and were studied by physicians of the greatest eminence; and to Greece these mysteries found their way from Oriental sources. But the school of cookery which the Romans introduced into Britain was gradually superseded in large measure by one more agreeable to the climate and physical demands of the people; and the free use of animal food, which was probably never a leading feature in the diet of the Italians as a community, and may be treated as an incidence of imperial luxury, proved not merely innocuous, but actually beneficial to a more northerly race.

So little is to be collected--in the shape of direct testimony, next to nothing--of the domestic life of the Britons--that it is only by conjecture that one arrives at the conclusion that the original diet of our countrymen consisted of vegetables, wild fruit, the honey of wild bees--which is still extensively used in this country,--a coarse sort of bread, and milk. The latter was evidently treated as a very precious article of consumption, and its value was enhanced by the absence of oil and the apparent want of butter. Mr. Ferguson supposes, from some remains of newly-born calves, that our ancestors sacrificed the young of the cow rather than submit to a loss of the milk; but it was, on the contrary, an early superstition, and may be, on obvious grounds, a fact, that the presence of the young increased the yield in the mother, and that the removal of the calf was detrimental. The Italian invaders augmented and enriched the fare, without, perhaps, materially altering its character; and the first decided reformation in the mode of living here was doubtless achieved by the Saxon and Danish settlers; for those in the south, who had migrated hither from the Low Countries, ate little flesh, and indeed, as to certain animals, cherished, according to Caesar, religious scruples against it.

It was to the hunting tribes, who came to us from regions even bleaker and more exacting than our own, that the southern counties owed the taste for venison and a call for some nourishment more sustaining than farinaceous substances, green stuff and milk, as well as a gradual dissipation of the prejudice against the hare, the goose, and the hen as articles of food, which the "Commentaries" record. It is characteristic of the nature of our nationality, however, that while the Anglo-Saxons and their successors refused to confine themselves to the fare which was more or less adequate to the purposes of archaic pastoral life in this island, they by no means renounced their partiality for farm and garden produce, but by a fusion of culinary tastes and experiences akin to fusion of race and blood, laid the basis of the splendid *cuisine* of the Plantagenet and Tudor periods. Our cookery is, like our tongue, an amalgam.

But the Roman historian saw little or nothing of our country except those portions which lay along or near the southern coast; the rest of his narrative was founded on hearsay; and he admits that the people in the interior--those beyond the range of his personal knowledge, more particularly the northern tribes and the Scots--were flesh-eaters, by which he probably intends, not consumers of cattle, but of the venison, game, and fish which abounded in their forests and rivers. The various parts of this country were in Caesar's day, and very long after, more distinct from each other for all purposes of communication and intercourse than we are now from Spain or from Switzerland; and the foreign influences which affected the South Britons made no mark on those petty states which lay at a distance, and whose diet was governed by purely local conditions. The dwellers northward were by nature hunters and fishermen, and became only by Act of Parliament poachers, smugglers, and illicit distillers; the province of the male portion of the family was to find food for the rest; and a pair of spurs laid on an empty trencher was well understood by the goodman as a token that the larder was empty and replenishable.

There are new books on all subjects, of which it is comparatively easy within a moderate compass to afford an intelligible, perhaps even a sufficient, account. But there are others which I, for my part, hesitate to touch, and which do not seem to be amenable to the law of selection. "Studies in Nidderland," by Mr. Joseph Lucas, is one of these. It was a labour of love, and it is full of records of singular survivals to our time of archaisms of all descriptions, culinary and gardening utensils not forgotten. There is one point, which I may perhaps advert to, and it is the square of wood with a handle, which the folk in that part of Yorkshire employed, in lieu of the ladle, for stirring, and the stone ovens for baking, which, the author tells us, occur also in a part of Surrey. But the volume should be read as a whole. We have of such too few.

Under the name of a Roman epicure, Coelius Apicius, has come down to us what may be accepted as the most ancient European "Book of Cookery." I think that the idea widely entertained as to this work having proceeded from the pen of a man, after whom it was christened, has no more substantial basis than a theory would have that the "Arabian Nights" were composed by Haroun al Raschid. Warner, in the introduction to his "Antiquitates Culinariae," 1791, adduces as a specimen of the rest two receipts from this collection, shewing how the Roman cook of the Apician epoch was wont to dress a hog's paunch, and to manufacture sauce for a boiled chicken. Of the three persons who bore the name, it seems to be thought most likely that the one who lived under Trajan was the true godfather of the Culinary Manual.

One of Massinger's characters (Holdfast) in the "City Madam," 1658, is made to charge the gourmets of his time with all the sins of extravagance perpetrated in their most luxurious and fantastic epoch. The object was to amuse the audience; but in England no "court gluttony," much less country Christmas, ever saw buttered eggs which had cost L30, or pies of carps' tongues, or pheasants drenched with ambergris, or sauce for a peacock made of the gravy of three fat wethers, or sucking pigs at twenty marks each.

Both Apicius and our Joe Miller died within L80,000 of being beggars--Miller something the nigher to that goal; and there was this community of insincerity also, that neither really wrote the books which carry their names. Miller could not make a joke or understand one when anybody else made it. His Roman foregoer, who would certainly never have gone for his dinner to Clare Market, relished good dishes, even if he could not cook them.

It appears not unlikely that the Romish clergy, whose monastic vows committed them to a secluded life, were thus led to seek some compensation for the loss of other worldly pleasures in those of the table; and that, when one considers the luxury of the old abbeys, one ought to recollect at the same time, that it was perhaps in this case as it was in regard to letters and the arts, and that we are under a certain amount of obligation to the monks for modifying the barbarism of the table, and encouraging a study of gastronomy.

There are more ways to fame than even Horace suspected. The road to immortality is not one but manifold. A man can but do what he can. As the poet writes and the painter fills with his inspiration the mute and void canvas, so doth the Cook his part. There was formerly apopular work in France entitled "Le Cuisinier Royal," by MM. Viard and Fouret, who describe themselves as "Hommes de Bouche." The twelfth edition lies before me, a thick octavo volume, dated 1805. The title-page is succeeded by an anonymous address to the reader, at the foot of which occurs a peremptory warning to pilferers of dishes or parts thereof; in other words, to piratical invaders of the copyright of Monsieur Barba. There is a preface equally unclaimed by signatures or initials, but as it is in the singular number the two hommes de bouche can scarcely have written it; perchance it was M. Barba aforesaid, lord-proprietor of these not-to-be-touched treasures; but anyhow the writer had a very sol-emn feeling of the debt which he had conferred on society by making the contents public for the twelfth time, and he concludes with a mixture of sentiments, which it is very difficult to define: "Dans la paix de ma conscience, non moins que dans l'orgueil d'avoir si honorablement rempli cette importante mission, je m'ecrierai avec le poete des gourmands et des amoureux:

"Exegi monumentum aere perennius Non omnis moriar."

THE EARLY ENGLISHMAN AND HIS FOOD.

William of Malmesbury particularly dwells on the broad line of distinction still existing between the southern English and the folk of the more northerly districts in his day, twelve hundred years after the visit of Caesar. He says that they were then (about A.D. 1150) as different as if they had been different races; and so in fact they were--different in their origin, in their language, and their diet.

In his "Folk-lore Relics of Early Village Life," 1883, Mr. Gomme devotes a chapter to "Early Domestic Customs," and quotes Henry's "History of Great Britain" for a highly curious clue to the primitive mode of dressing food, and partaking of it, among the Britons. Among the Anglo-Saxons the choice of poultry and game was fairly wide. Alexander Neckani, in his "Treatise on Utensils (twelfth century)" gives fowls, cocks, peacocks, the cock of the wood (the woodcock, not the capercailzie), thrushes, pheasants, and several more; and pigeons were only too plentiful. The hare and the rabbit were well enough known, and with the leveret form part of an enumeration of wild animals (animalium ferarum) in a pictorial vocabulary of the fifteenth century. But in the very early accounts or lists, although they must have soon been brought into requisition, they are not specifically cited as current dishes. How far this is attributable to the alleged repugnance of the Britons to use the hare for the table, as Caesar apprises us that they kept it only voluptatis causa, it is hard to say; but the way in which the author of the "Commentaries" puts it induces the persuasion that by *lepus* he means not the hare, but the rabbit, as the former would scarcely be domesticated.

Neckam gives very minute directions for the preparation of pork for the table.

He appears to have considered that broiling on the grill was the best way; the grid-iron had supplanted the hot stones or bricks in more fashionable households, and he recommends a brisk fire, perhaps with an eye to the skilful development of the crackling. He died without the happiness of bringing his archi-episcopal nostrils in contact with the sage and onions of wiser generations, and thinks that a little salt is enough. But, as we have before explained, Neckam prescribed for great folks. These refinements were unknown beyond the precincts of the palace and the castle.

In the ancient cookery-book, the "Menagier de Paris," 1393, which offers numerous points of similarity to our native culinary lore, the resources of the cuisine are represented as amplified by receipts for dressing hedgehogs, squirrels, magpies, and jackdaws--small deer, which the English experts did not affect, although I believe that the hedgehog is frequently used to this day by country folk, both here and abroad, and in India. It has white, rabbit-like flesh.

In an eleventh century vocabulary we meet with a tolerably rich variety of fish, of which the consumption was relatively larger in former times. The Saxons fished both with the basket and the net. Among the fish here enumerated are the whale (which was largely used for food), the dolphin, porpoise, crab, oyster, herring, cockle, smelt, and eel. But in the supplement to Alfric's vocabulary, and in another belonging to the same epoch, there are important additions to this list: the salmon, the trout, the lobster, the bleak, with the whelk and other shell-fish. But we do not notice the turbot, sole, and many other varieties, which became familiar in the next generation or so. The turbot and sole are indeed included in the "Treatise on Utensils" of Neckam, as are likewise the lamprey (of which King John is said to have been very fond), bleak, gudgeon, conger, plaice, limpet, ray, and mackerel.

The fifteenth century, if I may judge from a vocabulary of that date in Wright's collection, acquired a much larger choice of fish, and some of the names approximate more nearly to those in modern use. We meet with the sturgeon, the whiting, the roach, the miller's thumb, the thomback, the codling, the perch, the gudgeon, the turbot, the pike, the tench, and the haddock. It is worth noticing also that a distinction was now drawn between the fisherman and the fishmonger--the man who caught the fish and he who sold it--***piscator*** and ***piscarius***; and in the vocabulary itself the leonine line is cited: "Piscator prendit, quod piscarius bene vendit."

The whale was considerably brought into requisition for gastronomic purposes.

It was found on the royal table, as well as on that of the Lord Mayor of London. The cook either roasted it, and served it up on the spit, or boiled it and sent it in with peas; the tongue and the tail were favourite parts.

The porpoise, however, was brought into the hall whole, and was carved or **under-tranched** by the officer in attendance. It was eaten with mustard. The piece de resistance at a banquet which Wolsey gave to some of his official acquaintances in 1509, was a young porpoise, which had cost eight shillings; it was on the same occasion that His Eminence partook of strawberries and cream, perhaps; he is reported to have been the person who made that pleasant combination fashionable. The grampus, or sea-wolf, was another article of food which bears testimony to the coarse palate of the early Englishman, and at the same time may afford a clue to the partiality for disguising condiments and spices. But it appears from an entry in his Privy Purse Expenses, under September 8, 1498, that Henry the Seventh thought a porpoise a valuable commodity and a fit dish for an ambassador, for on that date twenty-one shillings were paid to Cardinal Morton's servant, who had procured one for some envoy then in London, perhaps the French representative, who is the recipient of a complimentary gratuity of L49 10s. on April 12, 1499, at his departure from England.

In the fifteenth century the existing stock of fish for culinary purposes received, if we may trust the vocabularies, a few accessions; as, for instance, the bream, the skate, the flounder, and the bake.

In "Piers of Fulham (14th century)," we hear of the good store of fat eels imported into England from the Low Countries, and to be had cheap by anyone who watched the tides; but the author reprehends the growing luxury of using the livers of young fish before they were large enough to be brought to the table.

The most comprehensive catalogue of fish brought to table in the time of Charles I. is in a pamphlet of 1644, inserted among my "Fugitive Tracts," 1875; and includes the oyster, which used to be eaten at breakfast with wine, the crab, lobster, sturgeon, salmon, ling, flounder, plaice, whiting, sprat, herring, pike, bream, roach, dace, and eel. The writer states that the sprat and herring were used in Lent. The sound of the stock-fish, boiled in wort or thin ale till they were tender, then laid on a cloth and dried, and finally cut into strips, was thought a good receipt for book-glue.

An acquaintance is in possession of an old cookery-book which exhibits the gamut of the fish as it lies in the frying-pan, reducing its supposed lament to musical notation. Here is an ingenious refinement and a delicate piece of irony, which Walton and Cotton might have liked to forestall.

The 15th century *Nominale* enriches the catalogue of dishes then in vogue. It specifies almond-milk, rice, gruel, fish-broth or soup, a sort of *fricassee* of fowl, collops, a pie, a pasty, a tart, a tartlet, a charlet (minced pork), apple-juice, a dish called jussell made of eggs and grated bread with seasoning of sage and saffron, and the three generic heads of sod or boiled, roast, and fried meats. In addition to the fish-soup, they had wine-soup, water-soup, ale-soup; and the flawn is reinforced by the *froise*. Instead of one Latin equivalent for a pudding, it is of moment to record that there are now three: nor should we overlook the rasher and the sausage. It is the earliest place where we get some of our familiar articles of diet--beef, mutton, pork, veal--under their modern names; and about the same time such terms present themselves as "a broth," "a browis," "a pottage," "a mess."

Of the dishes which have been specified, the *froise* corresponded to an omelette au lard of modern French cookery, having strips of bacon in it. The tansy was an omelette of another description, made chiefly with eggs and chopped herbs. As the former was a common dish in the monasteries, it is not improbable that it was one grateful to the palate. In Lydgate's "Story of Thebes," a sort of sequel to the "Canterbury Tales," the pilgrims invite the poet to join the supper-table, where there were these tasty omelettes: moile, made of marrow and grated bread, and haggis, which is supposed to be identical with the Scottish dish so called. Lydgate, who belonged to the monastery of Bury St. Edmunds, doubtless set on the table at Canterbury some of the dainties with which he was familiar at home; and this practice, which runs through all romantic and imaginative literature, constitutes, in our appreciation, its principal worth. We love and cherish it for its very sins against chronological and topographical fitness--its contempt of all unities. Men transferred local circumstances and a local colouring to their pictures of distant countries and manners. They argued the unknown from what they saw under their own eyes. They portrayed to us what, so far as the scenes and characters of their story went, was undeceivingly false, but what on the contrary, had it not been so, would never have been unveiled respecting themselves and their time.

The expenditure on festive occasions seems, from some of the entries in the "Northumberland Household Book," to present a strong contrast to the ordinary dietary allowed to the members of a noble and wealthy household, especially on fish days, in the earlier Tudor era (1512). The noontide breakfast provided for the Percy establishment was of a very modest character: my lord and my lady had, for example, a loaf of bread, two manchets (loaves of finer bread), a quart of beer and one of wine, two pieces of salt fish, and six baked herrings or a dish of sprats. My lord Percy and Master Thomas Percy had half a loaf of household bread, a manchet, a pottle of beer, a dish of butter, a piece of salt fish, and a dish of sprats or three white herrings; and the nursery breakfast for my lady Margaret and Master Ingram Percy was much the same. But on flesh days my lord and lady fared better, for they had a loaf of bread, two manchets, a quart of beer and the same of wine, and half a chine of mutton or boiled beef; while the nursery repast consisted of a manchet, a quart of beer, and three boiled mutton breasts; and so on: whence it is deducible that in the Percy family, perhaps in all other great houses, the members and the ladies and gentlemen in waiting partook of their earliest meal apart in their respective chambers, and met only at six to dine or sup.

The beer, which was an invariable part of the *menu*, was perhaps brewed from hops which, according to Harrison elsewhere quoted, were, after a long discontinuance, again coming into use about this time. But it would be a light-bodied drink which was allotted to the consumption at all events of Masters Thomas and Ingram Percy, and even of my Lady Margaret. It is clearly not irrelevant to my object to correct the general impression that the great families continued throughout the year to support the strain which the system of keeping open house must have involved. For, as Warner has stated, there were intervals during which the aristocracy permitted themselves to unbend, and shook off the trammels imposed on them by their social rank and responsibility. This was known as "keeping secret house," or, in other words, my lord became for a season incognito, and retired to one of his remoter properties for relaxation and repose. Our kings in some measure did the same; for they held their revels only, as a rule, at stated times and places. William I. is said to have kept his Easter at Winchester, his Whitsuntide at Westminster, and his Christmas at Gloucester. Even these antique grandees had to work on some plan. It could not be all mirth and jollity.

A recital of some of the articles on sale in a baker's or confectioner's shop in 1563, occurs in Newbery's "Dives Pragmaticus": simnels, buns, cakes, biscuits, comfits, caraways, and cracknels: and this is the first occurrence of the bun that I have hitherto been able to detect. The same tract supplies us with a few other items germane to my subject: figs, almonds, long pepper, dates, prunes, and nutmegs. It is curious to watch how by degrees the kitchen department was furnished with articles which nowadays are viewed as the commonest necessaries of life.

In the 17th century the increased communication with the Continent made us by degrees larger partakers of the discoveries of foreign cooks. Noblemen and gentlemen travelling abroad brought back with them receipts for making the dishes which they had tasted in the course of their tours. In the "Compleat Cook," 1655 and 1662, the beneficial operation of actual experience of this kind, and of the introduction of such books as the "Receipts for Dutch Victual" and "Epulario, or the Italian Banquet," to English readers and students, is manifest enough; for in the latter volume we get such entries as these: "To make a Portugal dish;" "To make a Virginia dish;" "A Persian dish;" "A Spanish olio;" and then there are receipts "To make a Posset the Earl of Arundel's way;" "To make the Lady Abergavenny's Cheese;" "The Jacobin's Pottage;" "To make Mrs. Leeds' Cheesecakes;" "The Lord Conway His Lordship's receipt for the making of Amber Puddings;" "The Countess of Rutland's receipt of making the Rare Banbury Cake, which was so much praised as her daughter's (the Right Honourable Lady Chaworth) Pudding," and "To make Poor Knights"--the last a medley in which bread, cream, and eggs were the leading materials.

Warner, however, in the "Additional Notes and Observations" to his "Antiquitates Culinariae," 1791, expresses himself adversely to the foreign systems of cookery from an English point of view. "Notwithstanding," he remarks, "the partiality of our countrymen to French cookery, yet that mode of disguising meat in this kingdom (except perhaps in the hottest part of the hottest season of the year) is an absurdity. It is *here* the art of spoiling good meat. The same art, indeed, in the South of France; where the climate is much warmer, and the flesh of the animal lean and insipid, is highly valuable; it is the art of making bad meat eatable." At the same time, he acknowledges the superior thrift and intelligence of the French cooks, and instances the frog and the horse. "The frog is considered in this country as a disgusting animal, altogether unfit for the purposes of the kitchen; whereas, by the efforts of French cookery, the thighs of this little creature are converted into a delicate and estimable dish." So sings, too (save the mark!), *our* Charles Lamb, so far back as 1822, after his visit to Paris. It seems that in Elizabeth's reign a *powdered*, or pickled horse was considered a suitable dish by a French general entertaining at dinner some English officers.

It is difficult to avoid an impression that Warner has some reason, when he suggests that the immoderate use of condiments was brought to us by the dwellers under a higher temperature, and was not really demanded in such a climate as that of England, where meat can be kept sweet in ordinary seasons, much longer even than in France or in Italy. But let us bear in mind, too, how different from our own the old English *cuisine* was, and how many strange beasts calling for lubricants it comprehended within its range.

An edifying insight into the old Scottish *cuisine* among people of the better sort is afforded by Fynes Morisoh, in his description of a stay at a knight's house in North Britain in 1598.

"Myself," he says, "was at a knight's house, who had many servants to attend him, that brought in his meat with their heads covered with blue caps, the table being more than half furnished with great platters of porridge, each having a little piece of sodden meat; and when the tables were served, the servants did sit down with us; but the upper mess, instead of porridge, had a pullet with some prunes in the broth. And I observed no art of cookery, or furniture of household stuff, but rather rude neglect of both, though myself and my companion, sent by the Governor of Berwick upon bordering affairs, were entertained in the best manner. The Scots ... vulgarly eat hearth-cakes of oats, but in cities have also wheaten bread, which, for the most part, was bought by courtiers, gentlemen, and the best sort of citizens. When I lived at Berwick, the Scots weekly upon the market day obtained leave in writing of the governor to buy peas and beans, whereof, as also of wheat, their merchants to this day (1617) send great quantities from London into Scotland. They drink pure wine, not with sugar, as the English, yet at feasts they put comfits in the wine, after the French manner: but they had not our vintners' fraud to mix their wines."

He proceeds to say that he noticed no regular inns, with signs hanging out, but that private householders would entertain passengers on entreaty, or where acquaintance was claimed. The last statement is interestingly corroborated by the account which Taylor the Water-Poet printed in 1618 of his journey to Scotland, and which he termed his "Penniless Pilgrimage or Moneyless Perambulation," in the course of which he purports to have depended entirely on private hospitality.

A friend says: "The Scotch were long very poor. Only their fish, oatmeal, and whiskey kept them alive. Fish was very cheap." This remark sounds the key-note of a great English want--cheaper fish. Of meat we already eat enough, or too much; but of fish we might eat more, if it could be brought at a low price to our doors. It is a noteworthy collateral fact that in the Lord Mayor of London's Pageant of 1590 there is a representation of the double advantage which would accrue if the unemployed poor were engaged to facilitate and cheapen the supply of fish to the City; and here we are, three centuries forward, with the want still very imperfectly answered.

Besides the bread and oatmeal above named, the bannock played its part. "The Land o' Cakes" was more than a trim and pretty phrase: there was in it a deep eloquence; it marked a wide national demand and supply.

The "Penny Magazine" for 1842 has a good and suggestive paper on "Feasts and Entertainments," with extracts from some of the early dramatists and a woodcut of "a new French cook, to devise fine kickshaws and toys." One curious point is brought out here in the phrase "boiled *jiggets* of mutton," which shews that the French *gigot* for a leg of mutton was formerly in use here. Like many other Gallicisms, it lingered in Scotland down to our own time.

The cut of the French cook above mentioned is a modern composition; and indeed some of the excerpts from Ben Jonson and other writers are of an extravagant and hyperbolical cast,--better calculated to amuse an audience than to instruct the student.

Mr. Lucas remarks: "It is probable that we are more dependent upon animal food than we used to be. In their early days, the present generation of dalesmen fed almost exclusively upon oatmeal; either as 'hasty-pudding,'--that is, Scotch oatmeal which had been ground over again, so as to be nearly as fine as flour;... or 'lumpy,'--that is, boiled quickly and not thoroughly stirred; or else in one of the three kinds of cake which they call 'fermented,' viz., 'riddle cake,' 'held-on cake,' or 'turn-down cake,' which is made from oatcake batter poured on the 'bak' ston" from the ladle, and then spread with the back of the ladle. It does not rise like an oatcake. Or of a fourth kind called 'clap cake.' They also made 'tiffany cakes' of wheaten flour, which was separated from the bran by being worked through a hair-sieve *tiffany*, or *temse*:--south of England *Tammy*,--with a brush called the Brush shank."

ROYAL FEASTS AND SAVAGE POMP.

In Rose's "School of Instructions for the Officers of the Mouth," 1682, the staff of a great French establishment is described as a Master of the Household, a Master Carver, a Master Butler, a Master Confectioner, a Master Cook, and a Master Pas-tryman. The author, who was himself one of the cooks in our royal kitchen, tells Sir Stephen Fox, to whom he dedicates his book, that he had entered on it after he had completed one of a very different nature: "The Theatre of the World, or a Prospect of Human Misery."

At the time that the "School of Instructions" was written, the French and our-selves had both progressed very greatly in the Art of Cookery and in the develop-ment of the *menu*. DelaHay Street, Westminster, near Bird-Cage Walk, suggests a time when a hedge ran along the western side of it towards the Park, in lieu of brick or stone walls; but the fact is that we have here a curious association with the office, just quoted from Rose, of Master Confectioner. For of the plot of ground on which the street, or at any rate a portion of it stands, the old proprieter was Peter DelaHaye, master confectioner of Charles II. at the very period of the publication of Rose's book. His name occurs in the title-deeds of one of the houses on the Park side, which since his day has had only five owners, and has been, since 1840, the freehold of an old and valued friend of the present writer.

It may be worth pointing out, that the Confectionery and Pastry were two distinct departments, each with its superintendent and staff. The fondness for con-fections had spread from Italy--which itself in turn borrowed the taste from the East--to France and England; and, as we perceive from the descriptions furnished in books, these were often of a very elaborate and costly character.

The volume is of the less interest for us, as it is a translation from the French, and consequently does not throw a direct light on our own kitchens at this period. But of course collaterally it presents many features of likeness and analogy, and may be compared with Braithwaite's earlier view to which I shall presently advert.

The following anecdote is given in the Epistle to Fox: "Many do believe the French way of working is cheapest; but let these examine this book, and then they may see (for their satisfaction) which is the best husbandry, to extract gold out of herbs, or to make a pottage of a stone, by the example of two soldiers, who in their quarters were minded to have a pottage; the first of them coming into a house and asking for all things necessary to the making of one, was as soon told that he could have none of these things there, whereupon he went away, and the other coming in with a stone in his knap-sack, asked only for a Pot to boil his stone in, that he might make a dish of broth of it for his supper, which was quickly granted him; and when the stone had boiled a little while, then he asked for a small bit of beef, then for a piece of mutton, and so for veal, bacon, etc., till by little and little he got all things requisite, and he made an excellent pottage of his stone, at as cheap a rate (it may be) as the cook extracted Gold from Herbs."

The kitchen-staff of a noble establishment in the first quarter of the seventeenth century we glean from Braithwaite's "Rules and Orders for the Government of the House of an Earl," which, if the "M.L." for whom the piece was composed was his future wife, Mistress Lawson, cannot have seen the light later than 1617, in which year they were married. He specifies--(1) a yeoman and groom for the cellar; (2) a yeoman and groom for the pantry; (3) a yeoman and groom for the buttery; (3a) a yeoman for the ewery; (4) a yeoman purveyor; (5) a master-cook, under-cooks, and three pastry-men; (6) a yeoman and groom in the scullery, one to be in the larder and slaughter-house; (7) an achator or buyer; (8) three conducts [query, errand-boys] and three kitchen-boys.

The writer also admits us to a rather fuller acquaintance with the mode in which the marketing was done. He says that the officers, among other matters, "must be able to judge, not only of the prices, but also of the goodness of all kinds of corn, cattle, and household provisions; and the better to enable themselves thereto, are oftentimes to ride to fairs and great markets, and there to have conference with graziers and purveyors." The higher officers were to see that the master was not deceived by purveyors and buyers, and that other men's cattle did not feed on my lord's pastures; they were to take care that the clerk of the kitchen kept his day-book "in that perfect and good order, that at the end of every week or month it be pied out," and that a true docket of all kinds of provisions be set down. They were to see that the powdered and salted meats in the larder were properly kept; and vigilant supervision was to be exercised over the cellar, buttery, and other departments, even to the prevention of paring the tallow lights.

Braithwaite dedicates a section to each officer; but I have only space to transcribe, by way of sample, the opening portion of his account of "The Officer of the Kitchen:" "The Master-Cook should be a man of years; well-experienced, whereby the younger cooks will be drawn the better to obey his directions. In ancient times noblemen contented themselves to be served with such as had been bred in their own houses, but of late times none could please some but Italians and Frenchmen, or at best brought up in the Court, or under London cooks: nor would the old manner of baking, boiling, and roasting please them, but the boiled meats must be after the French fashion, the dishes garnished about with sugar and preserved plums, the meat covered over with orangeade, preserved lemons, and with divers other preserved and conserved stuff fetched from the confectioner's: more lemons and sugar spent in boiling fish to serve at one meal than might well serve the whole expense of the house in a day." He goes on to describe and ridicule the new fashion of placing arms and crests on the dishes. It seems that all the refuse was the perquisite of the cook and his subordinates in a regulated proportion, and the same in the bakery and other branches; but, as may be supposed, in these matters gross abuses were committed.

In the "Leisure Hour" for 1884 was printed a series of papers on "English Homes in the Olden Times." The eleventh deals with service and wages, and is noticed here because it affords a recital of the orders made for his household by John Harington the elder in 1566, and renewed by John Harington the younger, his son and High Sheriff of Somersetshire, in 1592.

This code of domestic discipline for an Elizabethan establishment comprises the observance of decorum and duty at table, and is at least as valuable and curious as those metrical canons and precepts which form the volume (Babees' Book) edited for the Early English Text Society, etc.

There is rather too general a dislike on the part of antiquaries to take cognisance of matter inserted in popular periodicals upon subjects of an archaeological character; but of course the loose and flimsy treatment which this class of topics as a rule receives in the light literature of the day makes it perilous to use information so forthcoming in evidence or quotation. Articles must be rendered palatable to the general reader, and thus become worthless for all readers alike.

Most of the early descriptions and handbooks of instruction turn, naturally enough, on the demands and enjoyments of the great. There is in the treatise of Walter de Bibblesworth (14th century) a very interesting and edifying account of the arrangement of courses for some important banquet. The boar's head holds the place of honour in the list, and venison follows, and various dishes of roast. Among the birds to be served up we see cranes, peacocks, swans, and wild geese; and of the smaller varieties, fieldfares, plovers, and larks. There were wines; but the writer only particularises them as white and red. The haunch of venison was then an ordinary dish, as well as kid. They seem to have sometimes roasted and sometimes boiled them. Not only the pheasant and partridge appear, but the quail,--which is at present scarcer in this country, though so plentiful abroad,--the duck, and the mallard.

In connection with venison, it is worth while to draw attention to a passage in the "Privy Purse Expenses of Henry VII" where, under date of August 8, 1505, a woman receives 3s. *d*. for clarifying deer suet for the King. This was not for culinary but for medicinal purposes, as it was then, and much later, employed as an ointment.

Both William I. and his son the Red King maintained, as Warner shews us, a splendid table; and we have particulars of the princely scale on which an Abbot of Canterbury celebrated his installation in 1309. The archbishops of those times, if they exercised inordinate authority, at any rate dispensed in a magnificent manner among the poor and infirm a large portion of their revenues. They stood in the place of corporations and Poor Law Guardians. Their very vices were not without a certain fascinating grandeur; and the pleasures of the table in which our Plantagenet rulers outstripped even their precursors, the earlier sovereigns of that line, were enhanced and multiplied by the Crusades, by the commencing spirit of discovery, and by the foreign intermarriages, which became so frequent.

A far more thorough conquest than that which the day of Hastings signalised was accomplished by an army of a more pacific kind, which crossed the Channel piecemeal, bringing in their hands, not bows and swords, but new dishes and new wines. These invaders of our soil were doubtless welcomed as benefactors by the proud nobles of the Courts of Edward II. and Richard II., as well as by Royalty itself; and the descriptions which have been preserved of the banquets held on special occasions in the fourteenth and fifteenth centuries, and even of the ordinary style of living of some, make our City feasts of to-day shrink into insignificance. But we must always remember that the extravagant luxury and hospitality of the old time were germane and proper to it, component parts of the social framework.

It is to be remarked that some of the most disturbed and disastrous epochs in our annals are those to which we have to go for records of the greatest exploits in gastronomy and lavish expenditure of public money on comparatively unprofitable objects. During the period from the accession of Rufus to the death of Henry III., and again under the rule of Richard II., the taste for magnificent parade and sumptuous entertainments almost reached its climax. The notion of improving the condition of the poor had not yet dawned on the mind of the governing class; to make the artizan and the operative self-supporting and self-respectful was a movement not merely unformulated, but a conception beyond the parturient faculty of a member of the Jacquerie. The king, prince, bishop, noble, of unawakened England met their constituents at dinner in a fashion once or twice in a lifetime, and when the guests below the salt had seen the ways of greatness, they departed to fulfil their several callings. These were political demonstrations with a clear and (for the age) not irrational object; but for the modern public dinner, over which I should be happy to preach the funeral sermon, there is not often this or any other plea.

The redistribution of wealth and its diversion into more fruitful channels has already done something for the people; and in the future that lies before some of us they will do vastly more. All Augaea will be flushed out.

In some of these superb feasts, such as that at the marriage of Henry IV. in 1403, there were two series of courses, three of meat, and three of fish and sweets; in which we see our present fashion to a certain extent reversed. But at the coronation of Henry V. in 1421, only three courses were served, and those mixed. The taste for what were termed "subtleties," had come in, and among the dishes at this latter entertainment occur, "A pelican sitting on her nest with her young," and "an image of St. Catherine holding a book and disputing with the doctors." These vagaries became so common, that few dinners of importance were accounted complete without one or more.

One of the minor "subtleties" was a peacock in full panoply. The bird was first skinned, and the feathers, tail, head and neck having been laid on a table, and sprinkled with cummin, the body was roasted, glazed with raw egg-yolk, and after being left to cool, was sewn back again into the skin and so brought to table as the last course. In 1466, at the enthronement of Archbishop Nevile, no fewer than 104 peacocks were dressed.

The most extraordinary display of fish at table on a single occasion took place at the enthronement feast of Archbishop Warham in 1504; it occurred on a fast day; and consequently no meat, poultry or game was included in the *menu*, but ample compensation was found in the lavish assortment of confectionery, spices, beer and wine. Of wine of various vintages there were upwards of 12 pipes, and of ale and beer, thirty tuns, including four of London and six of Kentish ale.

The narratives which have descended to us of the prodigious banquets given on special occasions by our early kings, prelates and nobles, are apt to inspire the general reader with an admiration of the splendid hospitality of bygone times. But, as I have already suggested, these festivities were occasional and at long intervals, and during the intervening space the great ones and the small ones of mediaeval and early England did not indulge in this riotous sort of living, but "kept secret house," as it was called, both after their own fashion. The extremes of prodigality and squalor were more strongly marked among the poorer classes while this country was in a semi-barbarous condition, and even the aristocracy by no means maintained the same domestic state throughout the year as their modern representatives. There are not those ostentatious displays of wealth and generosity, which used to signalise certain political events, such as the coronation of a monarch or the enthronement of a primate; the mode of living has grown more uniform and consistent, since between the vilain and his lord has interposed himself the middle-class Englishman, with a hand held out to either.

A few may not spend so much, but as a people we spend more on our table. A good dinner to a shepherd or a porter was formerly more than a nine days' wonder; it was like a beacon seen through a mist. But now he is better fed, clothed and housed than the bold baron, whose serf he would have been in the good old days; and the bold baron, on his part, no longer keeps secret house unless he chooses, and observes, if a more monotonous, a more secure and comfortable tenor of life. This change is of course due to a cause which lies very near the surface--to the gradual effacement of the deeply-cut separating lines between the orders of society, and the stealthy uprise of the class, which is fast gathering all power into its own hands.

COOKERY BOOKS
PART 1.

The first attempt to illustrate this branch of the art must have been made by Alexander Neckam in the twelfth century; at least I am not aware of any older treatise in which the furniture and apparatus of a kitchen are set forth.

But it is needless to say that Neckam merely dealt with a theme, which had been familiar many centuries before his time, and compiled his treatise, "De Utensilibus," as Bishop Alfric had his earlier "Colloquy," with an educational, not a culinary, object, and with a view to facilitate the knowledge of Latin among his scholars. It is rather interesting to know that he was a native of St. Albans, where he was born in 1157. He died in 1217, so that the composition of this work of his (one of many) may be referred to the close of the twelfth century. Its value is, in a certain sense, impaired by the almost complete absence of English terms; Latin and (so called) Norman-French being the languages almost exclusively employed in it. But we have good reason indeed to be grateful for such a legacy in any shape, and when we consider the tendency of ways of life to pass unchanged from one generation to another, and when we think how many archaic and (to our apprehension) almost barbarous fashions and forms in domestic management lingered within living recollection, it will not be hazarding much after all to presume that the particulars so casually supplied to us by Neckam have an application alike before and after.

A student should also bear in mind that, from the strong Anglo-Gallic complexion of our society and manners in early days, the accounts collected by Lacroix are largely applicable to this country, and the same facilities for administering to the comfort and luxuries of the table, which he furnishes as illustrative of the gradual outgrowth from the wood fire and the pot-au-feu among his own countrymen, or certain classes of them, may be received as something like counterparts of what we possessed in England at or about the same period. We keep the phrase pot luck; but, for most of those who use it, it has parted with all its meaning. This said production of Neckam of St. Albans purports to be a guide to young housekeepers. It instructs them what they will require, if they desire to see their establishment well-ordered; but we soon perceive that the author has in view the arrangements indispensable for a family of high rank and pretensions; and it may be once for all observed that this kind of literature seldom proves of much service to us in an investigation of the state of the poor, until we come to the fifteenth or even sixteenth century, when the artists of Germany and the Low Countries began to delineate those scenes in industrial and servile life, which time and change have rendered so valuable.

Where their superiors in rank regarded them as little more than mechanical instruments for carrying on the business of life, the poor have left behind them few records of their mode of sustenance and of the food which enabled them to follow their daily toil. The anecdotes, whatever they may be worth, of Alfred and the burnt cakes, and of Tom Thumb's mamma and her Christmas pudding, made in a bowl, of which the principal material was pork, stand almost alone; for we get, wherever we look, nothing but descriptions by learned and educated men of their equals or betters, how they fed and what they ate--their houses, their furniture, their weapons, and their dress. Even in the passage of the old fabliau of the "King and the Hermit" the latter, instead of admitting us to a cottage interior, has a servant to wait on him, brings out a tablecloth, lights two candles, and lays before his disguised guest venison and wine. In most of our own romances, and in the epics of antiquity, we have to be satisfied with vague and splendid generalisations. We do not learn much of the dishes which were on the tables, how they were cooked, and how [Greek: oi polloi] cooked theirs.

The *Liber*, or rather Codex, Princeps in the very long and extensive catalogue of works on English Cookery, is a vellum roll called the Form of Cury, and is supposed to have been written about the beginning of the fifteenth century by the master-cook of Richard II who reigned from 1377 to 1399, and spent the public money in eating and drinking, instead of wasting it, as his grandfather had done, in foreign wars. This singular relic was once in the Harleian collection, but did not pass with the rest of the MSS. to the British Museum; it is now however, Additional MS. 5016, having been presented to the Library by Mr. Gustavus Brander. It was edited by Dr. Pegge in 1780, and included by Warner in his "Antiquitates Culinariae," 1791. The Roll comprises 196 receipts, and commences with a sort of preamble and a Table of Contents. In the former it is worth noting that the enterprise was undertaken "by the assent and avisement of masters of physic and of philosophy, that dwelled in his (Richard II.'s) court," which illustrates the ancient alliance between medicine and cookery, which has not till lately been dissolved. The directions were to enable a man "to make common pottages and common meats for the household, as they should be made, craftily and wholesomely;" so that this body of cookery was not prepared exclusively for the use of the royal kitchen, but for those who had not the taste or wish for what are termed, in contra-distinction, in the next sentence, "curious pottages, and meats, and subtleties." It is to be conjectured that copies of such a MS. were multiplied, and from time to time reproduced with suitable changes; but with the exception of two different, though nearly coeval, collections, embracing 31 and 162 receipts or nyms, and also successively printed by Pegge and Warner, there is no apparent trace of any systematic compilation of this nature at so remote a date.

The "Form of Cury" was in the 28 Eliz., in the possession of the Stafford family, and was in that year presented to the Queen by Edward, Lord Stafford, as is to be gathered from a Latin memorandum at the end, in his lordship's hand, preserved by Pegge and Warner in their editions. The fellowship between the arts of healing and cooking is brought to our recollection by a leonine verse at the end of one of the shorter separate collections above described:--

"Explicit de Coquina
   Quae est optima Medicina."

The "Form of Cury" will amply remunerate a study. It presents the earliest mention, so far as I can discern, of olive oil, cloves, mace, and gourds. In the receipts for making Aigredouce and Bardolf, sugar, that indispensable feature in the *cuisine*, makes its appearance; but it does so, I should add, in such a way as to lead to the belief that the use of sugar was at this time becoming more general. The difficulty, at first, seems to have been in refining it. We encounter here, too, onions under the name borrowed from the French instead of the Anglo-Saxon form "ynne leac"; and the prescriptions for making messes of almonds, pork, peas, and beans are numerous. There is "Saracen sauce," moreover, possibly as old as the Crusades, and pig with sage stuffing (from which it was but one step to duck). More than one species of "galantine" was already known; and I observe the distinction, in one of the smaller collections printed by Warner, between the tartlet formed of meat and the tartlet de fritures, of which the latter approaches more nearly our notion. The imperfect comprehension of harmonies, which is illustrated by the prehistoric bag-pudding of King Arthur, still continued in the unnatural union of flesh with sweets. It is now confined to the cottage, whence Arthur may have himself introduced it at Court and to the Knights of the Round Table.

In this authority, several of the dishes were to be cooked in white grease, which Warner interprets into *lard*; others demanded olive oil; but there is no allusion to butter. Among the receipts are some for dishes "in gravy"; rabbits and chickens were to be treated similarly; and the gravy appears to have consisted merely of the broth in which they were boiled, and which was flavoured with pounded almonds, powdered ginger, and sugar.

The "Liber Cure Cocorum," which is apparently extant only in a fifteenth century MS., is a metrical treatise, instructing its readers how to prepare certain dishes, condiments and accessories; and presents, for the most part, a repetition of what has already occurred in earlier and more comprehensive undertakings. It is a curious aid to our knowledge of the manner in which the table of the well-to-do Englishman was furnished in the time of Henry VI., and it is so far special, that it deals with the subject more from a middle-class point of view than the "Regulations for the Royal Household," and other similar compilations, which I have to bring under notice. The names, as usual, are often misleading, as in blanc manger, which is very different from our *blanc-mange*; and the receipt for "goose in a hog pot" leaves one in doubt as to its adaptability to the modern palate. The poetical ambition of the author has proved a source of embarrassment here and there; and in the receipt "for a service on a fish-day" the practitioner is prayed within four lines to cover his white herring for God's sake, and lay mustard over his red for God's love, because *sake* and *love* rhyme with *take* and *above*.

The next collection of receipts, which exists in a complete and homogeneous shape, is the "Noble Book of Cookery," of which an early MS. copy at Holkham was edited in 1882 by Mrs. Napier, but which had already been printed by Pynson in 1500, and subsequently by his successor, John Byddell. This interesting and important volume commences with a series of descriptions of certain royal and noble entertainments given on various occasions from the time of Henry IV. to that of Edward IV., and then proceeds to furnish a series of directions for the cook of a king's or prince's household; for, although both at the outset and the conclusion we are told that these dishes were calculated for all estates, it is abundantly obvious that they were such as never then, or very long subsequently, reached much lower than the court or the aristocracy. There is a less complete copy here of the feast at the enthronement of Archbishop Nevile. I regret that neither of the old printed copies is at present accessible. That of 1500 was formerly in the library at Bulstrode, and I was given by the late Mr. Bradshaw to understand that the same copy (no other being known) is probably at Longleat. By referring to Herbert's "Typographical Antiquities," anyone may see that, if his account (so far as it goes) is to be trusted, the printed copy varies from the Holkham MS. in many verbal particulars, and gives the date of Nevile's Feast as 1465.

The compilation usually known as the "Book of St. Albans," 1486, is, perhaps, next to the "Noble Book of Cookery," the oldest receptacle for information on the subject in hand. The former, however, deals with cookery only in an incidental and special way. Like Arnold's Chronicle, the St. Albans volume is a miscellany comprehending nearly all the matters that were apt to interest the few educated persons who were qualified to peruse its pages; and amid a variety of allied topics we come here across a catalogue of terms used in speaking of certain dishes of that day. The reference is to the prevailing methods of dressing and carving. A deer was said to be broken, a cony unlaced, a pheasant, partridge, or quail winged, a pigeon or a woodcock thighed, a plover minced, a mallard unbraced. They spoke of a salmon or a gurnard as chined, a sole as loined, a haddock as sided, an eel as trousoned, a pike as splatted, and a trout as gobbeted.

It must, I think, be predicated of Tusser's "Husbandry," of which the last edition published in the writer's lifetime is that of 1580, that it seems rather to reproduce precepts which occur elsewhere than to supply the reader with the fruits of his own direct observation. But there are certain points in it which are curious and original. He tells the ploughman that, after confession on Shrove Tuesday, he may go and thresh the fat hen, and if he is blindfold, kill her, and then dine on fritters and pancakes. At other times, seed-cakes, wafers, and other light confections.

It appears to have been usual for the farmer at that date to allow his hinds roast meat twice a week, on Sundays and on Thursday nights; but perhaps this was a generous extreme, as Tusser is unusually liberal in his ideas.

Tobias Venner, a Somersetshire man, brought out in 1620 his "Via Recta ad Vitam Longam." He was evidently a very intelligent person, and affords us the result of his professional experience and personal observation. He considered two meals a day sufficient for all ordinary people,--breakfast at eleven and supper at six (as at the universities); but he thought that children and the aged or infirm could not be tied by any rule. He condemns "bull's beef" as rank, unpleasant, and indigestible, and holds it best for the labourer; which seems to indicate more than anything else the low state of knowledge in the grazier, when Venner wrote: but there is something beyond friendly counsel where our author dissuades the poor from eating partridges, because they are calculated to promote asthma. "Wherefore," he ingenuously says, "when they shall chance to meet with a covey of young partridges, they were much better to bestow them upon such, for whom they are convenient!"

Salmon, turbot, and sturgeon he also reckoned hard of digestion, and injurious, if taken to excess; nor does he approve of herrings and sprats; and anchovies he characterises as the meat of drunkards. It is the first that we have heard of them.

He was not a bad judge of what was palatable, and prescribes as an agreeable and wholesome meal a couple of poached eggs with a little salt and vinegar, and a few corns of pepper, some bread and butter, and a draught of pure claret. He gives a receipt--the earliest I have seen in print--for making metheglin or hydromel. He does not object to furmety or junket, or indeed to custards, if they are eaten at the proper seasons, and in the middle or at the end of meals. But he dislikes mushrooms, and advises you to wash out your mouth, and rub your teeth and gums with a dry cloth, after drinking milk.

The potato, however, he praises as nutritious and pleasant to the taste, yet, as Gerarde the herbalist also says, flatulent. Venner refers to a mode of sopping them in wine as existing in his time. They were sometimes roasted in the embers, and there were other ways of dressing them. John Forster, of Hanlop, in Bucks, wrote a pamphlet in 1664 to shew that the more extended cultivation of this root would be a great national benefit.

Venner, who practised in the spring and autumn at Bath as a physician, had no relish for the poorer classes, who did not fare well at the hands of their superiors in any sense in the excellent old days. But he liked the Quality, in which he embraced the Universities, and he tenders them, among other little hints, the information that green ginger was good for the memory, and conserve of roses (not the salad of roses immortalised by Apuleius) was a capital posset against bed-time. "A conserve of rosemary and sage," says he, "to be often used by students, especially mornings fasting, doth greatly delight the brain."

The military ascendency of Spain did not fail to influence the culinary civilisation of those countries to which it temporarily extended its rule; and in a Venetian work entitled "Epulario, or the Italian Banquet," printed in 1549, we recognise the Spanish tone which had in the sixteenth century communicated itself to the cookery of the Peninsula, shewing that Charles V. and his son carried at least one art with them as an indemnity for the havoc which they committed.

The nursery rhyme of "Sing a song of sixpence" receives a singular and diverting illustration from the pages of this "Epulario," where occurs a receipt "to make Pies that the Birds may be alive in them, and fly out when it is cut up." Some of the other more salient beads relate to the mode of dressing sundry dishes in the Roman and Catalonian fashion, and teach us how to seethe gourds, as they did in Spain, and to make mustard after the manner of Padua.

I propose here to register certain contributions to our acquaintance with early culinary ideas and practices, which I have not specifically described:--

1. The Book of Carving. W. de Worde. 4to, 1508, 1513. Reprinted down to 1613.

2. A Proper New Book of Cookery. 12mo, 1546. Often reprinted. It is a recension of the "Book of Cookery," 1500.

3. The Treasury of Commodious Conceits and Hidden Secrets. By John Partridge. 12mo, 1580, 1586; and under the title of "Treasury of Hidden Secrets," 4to, 1596, 1600, 1637, 1653.

4. A Book of Cookery. Gathered by A.W. 12mo, 1584, 1591, etc.

5. The Good Housewife's Jewel. By Thomas Dawson. In two Parts, 12mo, 1585.

A copy of Part 2 of this date is in the British Museum.

6. The Good Housewife's Treasury. 12 mo, 1588.

7. Cookery for all manner of Dutch Victual. Licensed in 1590, but not otherwise known.

8. The Good Housewife's Handmaid for the Kitchen. 8vo, 1594.

9. The Ladies' Practice; or, a plain and easy direction for ladies and gentlewomen. By John Murrell. Licensed in 1617. Printed in 1621, and with additions in 1638, 1641, and 1650.

10. A Book of Cookery. By George Crewe. Licensed in 1623, but not known.

11. A Closet for Ladies and Gentlewomen. 12mo, 1630.

12. The Ladies' Cabinet Opened. By Patrick, Lord Ruthven. 4to, 1639; 8vo, 1655.

13. A Curious Treasury of Twenty Rare Secrets. Published by La Fountaine, an expert Operator. 4to, 1649.

14. A New Dispensatory of Fourty Physical Receipts. Published by Salvatore Winter of Naples, an expert Operator. 4to, 1649. Second edition, enlarged: same date.

The three last are rather in the class of miscellanies.

15. Health's Improvement; or, Rules comprising the discovering the Nature, Method, and Manner of preparing all sorts of Food used in this Nation. By Thomas Muffet (or Moffat), M.D. Corrected and enlarged by Christopher Bennett, M.D. 4to, 1655.

16. The Queen's Closet opened. Incomparable secrets in physick, chirurgery, Preserving, Candying, and Cookery.... Transcribed from the true copies of her Majesties own Receipt Books. By W.M., one of her late Servants.... London, 1655, 8vo. The same, corrected and revised, with many new and large Additions. 8vo, 1683.

17. The Perfect Cook: being the most exact directions for the making all kinds of pastes, with the perfect way teaching how to raise, season, and make all sorts of pies.... As also the Perfect English Cook.... To which is added the way of dressing all manner of Flesh. By M. Marmette. London, 1686, 12mo.

The writer of the "French Gardener," of which I have had occasion to say a good deal in my small volume on that subject, also produced, "Les Delices de la Campagne," which Evelyn excused himself from translating because, whatever experience he had in the garden, he had none, he says, in the shambles; and it was for those who affected such matters to get it done, but not by him who did the "French Cook"[1]. He seems to imply that the latter, though an excellent work in its way, had not only been marred in the translation, but was not so practically advantageous to us as it might have been, "for want of skill in the kitchen"--in other words, an evil, which still prevails, was then appreciated by intelligent observers--the English cook did not understand her business, and the English mistress, as a rule, was equally ignorant.

One of the engravings in the "French Gardener" represents women rolling out paste, preparing vegetables, and boiling conserves.

There is a rather quaint and attractive class of miscellaneous receipt-books, not made so on account of any particular merit in their contents, but by reason of their association with some person of quality. MS. Sloane 1367, is a narrow octavo volume, for instance, containing "My Lady Rennelagh's choice Receipts: as also some of Capt. Gvilt's, who valued them above gold." The value for us, however, is solely in the link with a noble family and the little touch about the Captain. There are many more such in public and private libraries, and they are often mere transcripts from printed works--select assemblages of directions for dressing food and curing diseases, formed for domestic reference before the advent of Dr. Buchan, and Mrs. Glasse, and Mrs. Rundell.

Among a valuable and extensive assemblage of English and foreign cookery books in the Patent Office Library, Mr. Ordish has obligingly pointed out to me a curious 4to MS., on the cover of which occurs, "Mrs. Mary Dacres her booke, 1666."

Even in the latter part of the seventeenth century the old-fashioned dishes, better suited to the country than to the Court taste, remained in fashion, and are included in receipt-books, even in that published by Joseph Cooper, who had been head-cook to Charles I, and who styles his 1654 volume "The Art of Cookery Refined and Augmented." He gives us two varieties of oatmeal pudding, French barley pudding, and hasty pudding in a bag. There is a direction for frying mushrooms, which were growing more into favour at the table than in the days when Castelve-

---

1   I have not seen this book, nor is it under that title in the catalogue of the British Museum

tri, whom I cite in my monograph on Gardening, was among us. Another dainty is an ox-palate pie.

Cooper's Preface is quaint, and surely modest enough. "Though the cheats," says he, "of some preceding pieces that treated on this subject (whose Title-pages, like the contents of a weekly Pamphlet, promised much more than the Books performed) may have provided this but a cold intertainment at its first coming abroad; yet I know it will not stay long in the world, before every rational reader will clear it of all alliance to those false pretenders. Ladies, forgive my confidence, if I tell you, that I know this piece will prove your favourite."

Yet Cooper's performance, in spite of its droll, self-complacent vein in the address to the Reader, is a judicious and useful selection, and was, in fact, far more serviceable to the middle-class gentry than some of those which had gone before. It adapted itself to sundry conditions of men; but it kept in view those whose purses were not richly lined enough to pay for dainties and "subtleties." It is pleasant to see that, after the countless centuries which had run out since Arthur, the bag-pudding and hot-pot maintained their ground--good, wholesome, country fare.

After the fall of the Monarchy in 1648, the chef de cuisine probably found his occupation gone, like a greater man before him; and the world may owe to enforced repose this condescension to the pen by the deposed minister of a king.

Soon after the Restoration it was that some Royalist brought out a small volume called "The Court and Kitchen of Elizabeth, commonly called Joan Cromwell, the wife of the late Usurper, truly described and represented," 12mo, 1664. Its design was to throw ridicule on the parsimony of the Protectoral household. But he recites some excellent dishes which made their appearance at Oliver's table: Dutch puddings, Scotch collops of veal, marrow puddings, sack posset, boiled woodcocks, and warden pies. He seems to have understood that eight stone of beef were cooked every morning for the establishment, and all scraps were diligently collected, and given alternately to the poor of St. Margaret's, Westminster, and St. Martin's-in-the-Fields. The writer acquaints us that, when the Protector entertained the French ambassador and the Parliament, after the Sindercome affair, he only spent L1,000 over the banquet, of which the Lady Protectress managed to save L200. Cromwell and his wife, we are told, did not care for suppers, but contented themselves with eggs and slops.

A story is told here of Cromwell and his wife sitting down to a loin of veal, and his calling for an orange, which was the sauce he preferred to that joint, and her highness telling him that he could not have one, for they were not to be had under a groat.

The Mansion House still retains the ancient usage of distributing the relics of a great feast afterwards among the poor, as Cromwell is said just above to have made a rule of his household. It was a practice highly essential in the absence of any organised system of relief.

The reign of Charles II., which witnessed a relationship with France of a very different character from that which the English maintained during the Plantagenet and earlier Tudor rule, was favourable to the naturalisation of the Parisian school of cookery, and numerous works were published at and about that time, in which the development of knowledge in this direction is shown to have taken place pari passu with the advance in gardening and arboriculture under the auspices of Evelyn.

In 1683 we come to a little volume entitled "The Young Cook's Monitor," by M.H., who made it public for the benefit of his (or her) scholars; a really valuable and comprehensive manual, wherein, without any attempt at arrangement, there is an ample assemblage of directions for preparing for the table all kinds of joints, made dishes, soups and broths, *frigacies*, puddings, pies, tarts, tansies, and jellies. Receipts for pickling are included, and two ways are shown how we should treat turnips after this wise. Some of the ingredients proposed for sauces seem to our ears rather prodigious. In one place a contemporary peruser has inserted an ironical calculation in MS. to the effect that, whereas a cod's head could be bought for fourpence, the condiments recommended for it were not to be had for less than nine shillings. The book teaches us to make Scotch collops, to pickle lemons and quinces, to make French bread, to collar beef, pork, or eels, to make gooseberry fool, to dry beef after the Dutch fashion, to make sack posset two ways, to candy flowers (violets, roses, etc.) for salads, to pickle walnuts like mangoes, to make flummery, to make a carp pie, to pickle French beans and cucumbers, to make damson and quince wines, to make a French pudding (called a Pomeroy pudding), to make a leg of pork like a Westphalia ham, to make mutton as beef, and to pot beef to eat like venison.

These and many other precepts has M.H. left behind him; and a sort of companion volume, printed a little before, goes mainly over the same ground, to wit,

"Rare and Excellent Receipts Experienced and Taught by Mrs. Mary Tillinghast, and now printed for the use of her scholars only," 1678. The lady appealed to a limited constituency, like M.H.; but her pages, such as they are (for there are but thirty), are now publici juris. The lesson to be drawn from Mistress Tillinghast's printed labours is that, among our ancestors in 1678, pies and pasties of all sorts, and sweet pastry, were in increased vogue. Her slender volume is filled with elucidations on the proper manufacture of paste of various sorts; and in addition to the pies designated by M.H. we encounter a Lombard pie, a Battalia pie, an artichoke pie, a potato (or secret) pie, a chadron[2] pie, and a herring pie. The fair author takes care to instruct us as to the sauces or dressings which are to accompany certain of her dishes.

"The Book of Cookery," 1500, of which there was a reprint by John Byddell about 1530 was often republished, with certain modifications, down to 1650, under the titles of "A Proper New Book of Cookery," or "The Book of Cookery." Notwithstanding the presence of many competitors, it continued to be a public favourite, and perhaps answered the wants of those who did not desire to see on their tables the foreign novelties introduced by travellers, or advertised in collections of receipts borrowed from other languages.

In fact, the first half of the seventeenth century did not witness many accessions to the store of literature on this subject. But from the time of the Commonwealth, the supply of works of reference for the housekeeper and the cook became much more regular and extensive. In 1653, Selden's friend, the Countess of Kent, brought out her "Choice Manual of Physic and Chirurgery," annexing to it receipts for preserving and candying; and there were a few others, about the same time, of whose works I shall add here a short list:--

1. The Accomplished Cook. By Robert May. 8vo, 1660. Fifth edition, 8vo, 1685.

2. The Whole Body of Cookery Dissected. By Will. Rabisha. 8vo, 1661.

3. The Queen-like Closet: a Rich Cabinet, stored with all manner of rare receipts. By Hannah Wolley. 8vo, 1670.

4. The True Way of Preserving and Candying, and making several sorts of Sweetmeats. Anon. 8vo, 1681.

---

2 A pie chiefly composed of a calf's chadroa

5. The Complete Servant-Maid. 12 mo, 1682-3.

6. A Choice Collection of Select Remedies.... Together with excellent Directions for Cooking, and also for Preserving and Conserving. By G. Hartman [a Chemist]. 8vo, 1684.

7. A Treatise of Cleanness in Meats and Drinks, of the Preparation of Food, etc. By Thomas Tryon. 4to, 1682.

8. The Genteel Housekeeper's Pastime; or, The mode of Carving at the Table represented in a Pack of Playing Cards. 8vo, 1693.

9. A New Art of Brewing Beer, Ale, and other sorts of Liquors. By T. Tryon. 12mo, 1690-91.

10. The Way to get Wealth; or, A New and Ready Way to make twenty-three sorts of Wines, equal to that of France ... also to make Cyder.... By the same. 12mo, 1702.

11. A Treatise of Foods in General. By Louis Lemery. Translated into English. 8vo, 1704.

12. England's Newest Way in all sorts of Cookery. By Henry Howard, Free Cook of London. Second edition, 8vo, 1708.

13. Royal Cookery; or, the Complete Court-Cook. By Patrick Lamb, Esq., near 50 years Master-Cook to their late Majesties King Charles II., King James II., King William, Mary, and to her present Majesty, Queen Anne. 8vo, 1710. Third edition, 8vo, 1726.

14. The Queen's Royal Cookery. By J. Hall, Free Cook of London. 12mo, 1713-15.

15. Mrs. Mary Eales' Receipts, Confectioner to her late Majesty, Queen Anne. 8vo, 1718.

16. A Collection of three hundred Receipts in Cookery, Physic, and Surgery. In two parts, 8vo, 1729.

17. The Complete City and Country Cook. By Charles Carter. 8vo, 1732.

18. The Complete Housewife. Seventh edition, 8vo, 1736.

19. The Complete Family Piece: A very choice Collection of Receipts. Second edition, 8vo, 1737.

20. The Modern Cook. By Vincent La Chapelle, Cook to the Prince of Orange. Third edition. 8vo, 1744.

21. A Treatise of all sorts of Foods. By L. Lemery. Translated by D. Hay, M.D. 8vo, 1745.

This completes the list of books, so far as they have fallen in my way, or been pointed out by the kindness of friends, down to the middle of the last century.

It was probably Charles, Duke of Bolton (1698-1722), who was at one time Lord-Lieutenant of Ireland, and who in the beginning of his ducal career, at all events, resided in St. James's Street, that possessed successively as head-cooks John Nott and John Middleton. To each of these artists we owe a volume of considerable pretensions, and the "Cook's and Confectioner's Dictionary," 1723, by the former, is positively a very entertaining and cyclopedic publication. Nott inscribes his book "To all Good Housewives," and declares that he placed an Introduction before it merely because fashion had made it as strange for a book to appear without one as for a man to be seen in church without a neckcloth or a lady without a hoop-petti-coat. He congratulates himself and his readers on living in a land flowing with milk and honey, quotes the saw about God sending meat and somebody else sending cooks, and accounts for his omission of pigments by saying, like a gallant man, that his countrywomen little needed such things. Nott opens with Some Divertisements in Cookery, us'd at Festival-Times, as Twelfth-Day, etc., which are highly curi-ous, and his dictionary itself presents the novelty of being arranged, lexicon-wise, alphabetically. He seems to have been a fairly-read and intelligent man, and cites, in the course of his work, many celebrated names and receipts. Thus we have:--To brew ale Sir Jonas Moore's way; to make Dr. Butler's purging ale; ale of health and strength, by the Viscount St. Albans; almond butter the Cambridge way; to dress a leg of mutton a la Dauphine; to dress mutton the Turkish way; to stew a pike the City way. Dr. Twin's, Dr. Blacksmith's, and Dr. Atkin's almond butter; an amber pudding, according to the Lord Conway's receipt; the Countess of Rutland's Ban-bury cake; to make Oxford cake; to make Portugal cakes; and so on. Nott embraces every branch of his subject, and furnishes us with bills of fare for every month of the year, terms and rules of carving, and the manner of setting out a dessert of fruits and sweetmeats. There is a singular process explained for making China broth, into which an ounce of china is to enter. Many new ways had been gradually found of utilising the materials for food, and vegetables were growing more plentiful. The carrot was used in soups, puddings, and tarts. Asparagus and spinach, which are wanting in all the earlier authorities, were common, and the barberry had come into favour. We now begin to notice more frequent mention of marmalades, blanc-manges, creams, biscuits, and sweet cakes. There is a receipt for a carraway cake, for a cabbage pudding, and for a chocolate tart.

The production by his Grace of Bolton's other *chef*, John Middleton, is "Five Hundred New Receipts in Cookery, Confectionary, Pastry, Preserving, Conserving, Pickling," and the date is 1734. Middleton doubtless borrowed a good deal from his predecessor; but he also appears to have made some improvements in the science. We have here the methods, to dress pikes a la sauce Robert, to make blackcaps (apples baked in their skins); to make a Wood Street cake; to make Shrewsbury cakes; to dress a leg of mutton like a gammon of bacon; to dress eggs a la Augemotte; to make a dish of quaking pudding of several colours; to make an Italian pudding, and to make an Olio. The eye seems to meet for the first time with hasty pudding, plum-porridge (an experiment toward the solidification of the older plum-broth), rolled beef-steaks, samphire, hedgehog cream (so called from its shape, currants be-ing used for the eyes, and cut almonds for the bristles), cocks'-combs, orange, spin-ach and bean tarts, custards in cups (the 1723 book talks of jellies served on china plates), and lastly, jam--the real jam of these days, made to last, as we are told, the whole year. There is an excellent prescription for making elderberry wine, besides, in which Malaga raisins are to be largely used. "In one year," says our *chef*, "it will be as good and as pleasant as French wine."

Let us extract the way "to make Black-caps":--"Take a dozen of good pippins, cut them in halves, and take out the cores; then place them on a right Mazarine dish with the skins on, the cut side downwards; put to them a very little water, scrape on them some loaf sugar, put them in a hot oven till the skins are burnt black, and your apples tender; serve them on Plates strew'd over with sugar."

Of these books, I select the preface to "The Complete Housewife," by E. Smith, 1736, because it appears to be a somewhat more ambitious endeavour in an intro-ductory way than the authors of such undertakings usually hazard. From the last paragraph we collect that the writer was a woman, and throughout she makes us aware that she was a person of long practical experience. Indeed, as the volume comprehends a variety of topics, including medicines, Mrs. or Miss Smith must have been unusually observant, and have had remarkable opportunities of making herself conversant with matters beyond the ordinary range of culinary specialists. I propose presently to print a few samples of her workmanship, and a list of her principal receipts in that section of the book with which I am just now concerned. First of all, here is the Preface, which begins, as we see, by a little piece of plagiarism from Nott's exordium:--

"*PREFACE.*

"It being grown as unfashionable for a book now to appear in publick without a preface, as for a lady to appear at a ball without a hoop-petticoat, I shall conform to custom for fashion-sake, and not through any necessity. The subject being both common and universal, needs no arguments to introduce it, and being so necessary for the gratification of the appetite, stands in need of no encomiums to allure persons to the practice of it; since there are but few now-a-days who love not good eating and drinking. Therefore I entirely quit those two topicks; but having three or four pages to be filled up previous to the subject it self, I shall employ them on a subject I think new, and not yet handled by any of the pretenders to the art of cookery; and that is, the antiquity of it; which if it either instruct or divert, I shall be satisfied, if you are so.

"Cookrey, confectionary, &c., like all other sciences and arts, had their infancy, and did not arrive at a state of maturity but by slow degrees, various experiments, and a long tract of time: for in the infant-age of the world, when the new inhabitants contented themselves with the simple provision of nature, viz. the vegetable diet, the fruits and production of the teeming ground, as they succeeded one another in their several peculiar seasons, the art of cookery was unknown; apples, nuts, and herbs, were both meat and sauce, and mankind stood in no need of any additional sauces, ragoes, &c., but a good appetite; which a healthful and vigorous constitution, a clear, wholesome, odoriferous air, moderate exercise, and an exemption from anxious cares, always supplied them with.

"We read of no palled appetites, but such as proceeded from the decays of nature by reason of an advanced old age; but on the contrary a craving stomach, even upon a death-bed, as in Isaac: nor no sicknesses but those that were both the first and the last, which proceeded from the struggles of nature, which abhorred the dissolution of soul and body; no physicians to prescribe for the sick, nor no apothecaries to compound medicines for two thousand years and upwards. Food and physick were then one and the same thing.

"But when men began to pass from a vegetable to an animal diet, and feed on flesh, fowls, and fish, then seasonings grew necessary, both to render it more palatable and savoury, and also to preserve that part which was not immediately spent from stinking and corruption: and probably salt was the first seasoning discover'd; for of salt we read, Gen. xiv.

"And this seems to be necessary, especially for those who were advanced in age, whose palates, with their bodies, had lost their vigour as to taste, whose digestive faculty grew weak and impotent; and thence proceeded the use of soops and savoury messes; so that cookery then began to become a science, though luxury had not brought it to the height of an art. Thus we read, that Jacob made such palatable pottage, that Esau purchased a mess of it at the extravagant price of his birthright. And Isaac, before by his last will and testament he bequeathed his blessing to his son Esau, required him to make some savoury meat, such as his soul loved, i.e., such as was relishable to his blunted palate.

"So that seasonings of some sort were then in use; though whether they were salt, savoury herbs, or roots only; or spices, the fruits of trees, such as pepper, cloves, nutmeg; bark, as cinnamon; roots, as ginger, &c., I shall not determine.

"As for the methods of the cookery of those times, boiling or stewing seems to have been the principal; broiling or roasting the next; besides which, I presume scarce any other were used for two thousand years and more; for I remember no other in the history of Genesis.

"That Esau was the first cook, I shall not presume to assert; for Abraham gave order to dress a fatted calf; but Esau is the first person mentioned that made any advances beyond plain dressing, as boiling, roasting, &c. For though we find indeed, that Rebecca his mother was accomplished with the skill of making savoury meat as well as he, yet whether he learned it from her, or she from him, is a question too knotty for me to determine.

"But cookery did not long remain a simple science, or a bare piece of housewifry or family ceconomy, but in process of time, when luxury entered the world, it grew to an art, nay a trade; for in I Sam. viii. 13. when the Israelites grew fashionists, and would have a king, that they might be like the rest of their neighbours, we read of cooks, confectioners, &c.

"This art being of universal use, and in constant practice, has been ever since upon the improvement; and we may, I think, with good reason believe, is arrived at its greatest height and perfection, if it is not got beyond it, even to its declension; for whatsoever new, upstart, out-of-the-way messes some humourists have invented, such as stuffing a roasted leg of mutton with pickled herring, and the like, are only the sallies of a capricious appetite, and debauching rather than improving the art itself.

"The art of cookery, &c., is indeed diversified according to the diversity of nations or countries; and to treat of it in that latitude would fill an unportable volume; and rather confound than improve those that would accomplish themselves with it. I shall therefore confine what I have to communicate within the limits of practicalness and usefulness, and so within the compass of a manual, that shall neither burthen the hands to hold, the eyes in reading, nor the mind in conceiving.

"What you will find in the following sheets, are directions generally for dressing after the best, most natural, and wholesome manner, such provisions as are the product of our own country, and in such a manner as is most agreeable to English palates: saving that I have so far temporized, as, since we have to our disgrace so fondly admired the French tongue, French modes, and also French messes, to present you now and then with such receipts of French cookery, as I think may not be disagreeable to English palates.

"There are indeed already in the world various books that treat on this subject, and which bear great names, as cooks to kings, princes, and noblemen, and from which one might justly expect something more than many, if not most of these I have read, perform, but found my self deceived in my expectations; for many of them to us are impracticable, others whimsical, others unpalatable, unless to depraved palates; some unwholesome, many things copied from old authors, and recommended without (as I am persuaded) the copiers ever having had any experience of the palatableness, or had any regard to the wholesomness of them; which two things ought to be the standing rules, that no pretenders to cookery ought to deviate from. And I cannot but believe, that those celebrated performers, notwithstanding all their professions of having ingenuously communicated their art, industriously concealed their best receipts from the publick.

"But what I here present the world with is the product of my own experience, and that for the space of thirty years and upwards; during which time I have been constantly employed in fashionable and noble families, in which the provisions ordered according to the following directions, have had the general approbation of such as have been at many noble entertainments.

"These receipts are all suitable to English constitutions and English palates, wholesome, toothsome, all practicable and easy to be performed. Here are those proper for a frugal, and also for a sumptuous table, and if rightly observed, will prevent the spoiling of many a good dish of meat, the waste of many good materials, the vexation that frequently attends such mismanagements, and the curses not unfrequently bestowed on cooks with the usual reflection, that whereas God sends good meat, the devil sends cooks.

"As to those parts that treat of confectionary, pickles, cordials, English wines, &c., what I have said in relation to cookery is equally applicable to them also.

"It is true, I have not been so numerous in receipts as some who have gone before me, but I think I have made amends in giving none but what are approved and practicable, and fit either for a genteel or a noble Table; and altho' I have omitted odd and fantastical messes, yet I have set down a considerable number of receipts.

"The treatise is divided into ten parts: cookery contains above an hundred receipts, pickles fifty, puddings above fifty, pastry above forty, cakes forty, creams and jellies above forty, preserving an hundred, made wines forty, cordial waters and powders above seventy, medicines and salves above two hundred; in all near eight hundred.

"I have likewise presented you with schemes engraven on copper-plates for the regular disposition or placing the dishes of provision on the table according to the best manner, both for summer and winter, first and second courses, &c.

"As for the receipts for medicines, salves, ointments, good in several diseases, wounds, hurts, bruises, aches, pains, &c., which amount to above two hundred, they are generally family receipts, that have never been made publick; excellent in their kind, and approved remedies, which have not been obtained by me without much difficulty; and of such efficacy in distempers, &c., to which they are appropriated, that they have cured when all other means have failed; and a few of them which I have communicated to a friend, have procured a very handsome livelihood.

"They are very proper for those generous, charitable, and Christian gentlewomen that have a disposition to be serviceable to their poor country neighbours, labouring under any of the afflicted circumstances mentioned; who by making the medicines, and generously contributing as occasions offer, may help the poor in their afflictions, gain their good-will and wishes, entitle themselves to their blessings and prayers, and also have the pleasure of seeing the good they do in this world, and have good reason to hope for a reward (though not by way of merit) in the world to come.

"As the whole of this collection has cost me much pains and a thirty years' diligent application, and I have had experience of their use and efficacy, I hope they will be as kindly accepted, as by me they are generously offered to the publick: and if they prove to the advantage of many, the end will be answered that is proposed by her that is ready to serve the publick in what she may."

COOKERY BOOKS.
PART II.
SELECT EXTRACTS FROM AN
EARLY RECEIPT-BOOK.

The earliest school of English Cookery, which had such a marked Anglo-Norman complexion, has been familiarised to us by the publication of Warner's Antiquitates Culinaricae, 1791, and more recently by the appearance of the "Noble Book of Cookery" in Mrs. Napier's edition, not to mention other aids in the same way, which are accessible; and it seemed to be doing a better service, when it became a question of selecting a few specimens of old receipts, to resort to the representative of a type of culinary philosophy and sentiment somewhere midway between those which have been rendered easy of reference and our own. I have therefore given in the few following pages, in a classified shape, some of the highly curious contents of E. Smith's "Compleat Housewife," 1736, which maybe securely taken to exhibit the state of knowledge in England upon this subject in the last quarter of the seventeenth century and first quarter of the succeeding one. In the work itself no attempt at arrangement is offered.

I.--MEAT, POULTRY, ETC.

To make Dutch-beef:--Take the lean part of a buttock of beef raw; rub it well with brown sugar all over, and let it lie in a pan or tray two or three hours, turning it three or four times; then salt it well with common salt and salt-petre, and let it lie a fortnight, turning it every day; then roll it very strait in a coarse cloth, and put it in a cheese-press a day and a night, and hang it to dry in a chimney. When you boil it, you must put it in a cloth: when 'tis cold, it will cut out into shivers as Dutch-beef.

To dry Mutton to cut out in Shivers as Dutch-Beef:--Take a middling leg of mutton, then take half a pound of brown sugar, and rub it hard all over your mutton, and let it lie twenty-four hours; then take an ounce and half of saltpetre, and mix it with a pound of common salt, and rub that all over the mutton every other day, till 'tis all on, and let it lie nine days longer; keep the place free from brine, then hang it up to dry three days, then smoke it in a chimney where wood is burnt; the fire must not be too hot; a fortnight will dry it. Boil it like other hams, and when 'tis cold, cut it out in shivers like Dutch-beef.

To stuff a Shoulder or Leg of Mutton with Oysters:--Take a little grated bread, some beef-suet, yolks of hard eggs, three anchovies, a bit of an onion, salt and pepper, thyme and winter-savoury, twelve oysters, some nutmeg grated; mix all these together, and shred them very fine, and work them up with raw eggs like a paste, and stuff your mutton under the skin in the thickest place, or where you please, and roast it; and for sauce take some of the oyster-liquor, some claret, two or three anchovies, a little nutmeg, a bit of an onion, the rest of the oysters: stew all these together, then take out the onion, and put it under the mutton.

To marinade a Leg of Lamb:--Take a leg of lamb, cut it in pieces the bigness of a half-crown; hack them with the back of a knife; then take an eschalot, three or four anchovies, some cloves, mace, nutmeg, all beaten; put your meat in a dish, and strew the seasoning over it, and put it in a stew-pan, with as much white-wine as will cover it, and let it be two hours; then put it all together in a frying-pan, and let it be half enough; then take it out and drain it through a colander, saving the liquor, and put to your liquor a little pepper and salt, and half a pint of gravy; dip your meat in yolks of eggs, and fry it brown in butter; thicken up your sauce with yolks of eggs and butter, and pour it in the dish with your meat: lay sweet-breads and forc'd-meat balls over your meat; dip them in eggs, and fry them. Garnish with lemon.

A Leg of Mutton a-la-Daube:--Lard your meat with bacon through, but slant-way; half roast it; take it off the spit, and put it in a small pot as will boil it; two quarts of strong broth, a pint of white-wine, some vinegar, whole spice, bay-leaves, green onions, savoury, sweet-marjoram; when 'tis stew'd enough, make sauce of some of the liquor, mushrooms, lemon cut like dice, two or three anchovies: thicken it with browned butter. Garnish with lemon.

To fry Cucumbers for Mutton Sauce:--You must brown some butter in a pan, and cut the cucumbers in thin slices; drain them from the water, then fling them into the pan, and when they are fried brown, put in a little pepper and salt, a bit of an onion and gravy, and let them stew together, and squeeze in some juice of lemon; shake them well, and put them under your mutton.

To make Pockets:--Cut three slices out of a leg of veal, the length of a finger, the breadth of three fingers, the thickness of a thumb, with a sharp penknife; give it a slit through the middle, leaving the bottom and each side whole, the thickness of a straw; then lard the top with small fine lards of bacon; then make a forc'd-meat of marrow, sweet-breads, and lamb-stones just boiled, and make it up after 'tis seasoned and beaten together with the yolks of two eggs, and put it into your pockets as if you were filling a pincushion; then sew up the top with fine thread, flour them, and put melted butter on them, and bake them; roast three sweet-breads to put between, and serve them with gravy-sauce.

To make a Florendine of Veal:--Take the kidney of a loin of veal, fat and all, and mince it very fine; then chop a few herbs, and put to it, and add a few currants; season it with cloves, mace, nutmeg, and a little salt; and put in some yolks of eggs, and a handful of grated bread, a pippin or two chopt, some candied lemon-peel minced small, some sack, sugar, and orange-flower-water. Put a sheet of puff-paste at the bottom of your dish; put this in, and cover it with another; close it up, and when 'tis baked, scrape sugar on it; and serve it hot.

To make a Tureiner:--Take a china pot or bowl, and fill it as follows: at the bottom lay some fresh butter; then put in three or four beef-steaks larded with bacon; then cut some veal-steaks from the leg; hack them, and wash them over with the yolk of an egg, and afterwards lay it over with forc'd-meat, and roll it up, and lay it in with young chickens, pigeons and rabbets, some in quarters, some in halves; sweet-breads, lamb-stones, cocks-combs, palates after they are boiled, peeled, and cut in slices: tongues, either hogs or calves, sliced, and some larded with bacon: whole yolks of hard eggs, pistachia-nuts peeled, forced balls, some round, some like an olive, lemon sliced, some with the rind on, barberries and oysters: season all these with pepper, salt, nutmeg, and sweet-herbs, mix'd together after they are cut very small, and strew it on every thing as you put it in your pot: then put in a quart of gravy, and some butter on the top, and cover it close with a lid of puff-paste, pretty thick. Eight hours will bake it.

To make Hams of Pork like Westphalia:--To two large hams, or three small ones, take three pounds of common salt, and two pounds and half of brown coarse sugar; mix both together, and rub it well into the hams, and let them lie seven days, turning them every day, and rub the salt in them, when you turn them; then take four ounces of salt-petre beat small, and mix with two handfuls of common salt, and rub that well in your hams, and let them lie a fortnight longer: then hang them up high in a chimney to smoke.

To make a Ragoo of Pigs-Ears:--Take a quantity of pigs-ears, and boil them in one half wine and the other water; cut them in small pieces, then brown a little butter, and put them in, and a pretty deal of gravy, two anchovies, an eschalot or two, a little mustard, and some slices of lemon, some salt, and nutmeg; stew all these together, and shake it up thick. Garnish the dish with barberries.

To collar a Pig:--Cut off the head of your pig; then cut the body asunder; bone it, and cut two collars off each side; then lay it in water to take out the blood; then take sage and parsley, and shred them very small, and mix them with pepper, salt, and nutmeg, and strew some on every side, or collar, and roll it up, and tye it with coarse tape; so boil them in fair water and salt, till they are very tender: put two or three blades of mace in the kettle, and when they are enough, take them up, and lay them in something to cool; strain out some of the liquor, and add to it some vinegar and salt, a little white-wine, and three or four bay-leaves; give it a boil up, and when 'tis cold put it to the collars, and keep them for use.

A Fricasy of Double Tripe:--Cut your tripe in slices, two inches long, and put it into a stew-pan; put to it a quarter of a pound of capers, as much samphire shred, half a pint of strong broth, as much white-wine, a bunch of sweet-herbs, a lemon shred small; stew all these together till 'tis tender; then take it off the fire, and thicken up the liquor with the yolks of three or four eggs, a little parsley boiled green and chopp'd, some grated nutmeg and salt; shake it well together. Serve it on sippets. Garnish with lemon.

To pot a Swan:--Bone and skin your swan, and beat the flesh in a mortar, taking out the strings as you beat it; then take some clear fat bacon, and beat with the swan, and when 'tis of a light flesh colour, there is bacon enough in it; and when 'tis beaten till 'tis like dough, 'tis enough; then season it with pepper, salt, cloves, mace, and nutmeg, all beaten fine; mix it well with your flesh, and give it a beat or two all together; then put it in an earthen pot, with a little claret and fair water, and at the top two pounds of fresh butter spread over it; cover it with coarse paste, and bake it with bread; then turn it out into a dish, and squeeze it gently to get out the moisture; then put it in a pot fit for it; and when 'tis cold, cover it over with clarified butter, and next day paper it up. In this manner you may do goose, duck, or beef, or hare's flesh.

To make a Poloe:--Take a pint of rice, boil it in as much water as will cover it; when your rice is half boiled, put in your fowl, with a small onion, a blade or two of mace, some whole pepper, and some salt; when 'tis enough, put the fowl in the dish, and pour the rice over it.

To make a Pulpatoon of Pigeons:--Take mushrooms, palates, oysters, sweet-breads, and fry them in butter; then put all these into a strong gravy; give them a heat over the fire, and thicken up with an egg and a bit of butter; then half roast six or eight pigeons, and lay them in a crust of forc'd-meat as follows: scrape a pound of veal, and two pounds of marrow, and beat it together in a stone mortar, after 'tis shred very fine; then season it with salt, pepper, spice, and put in hard eggs, anchovies and oysters; beat all together, and make the lid and sides of your pye of it; first lay a thin crust into your pattipan, then put on your forc'd-meat; then lay an exceeding thin crust over them; then put in your pigeons and other ingredients, with a little butter on the top. Bake it two hours.

To keep Green Peas till Christmas:--Shell what quantity you please of young peas; put them in the pot when the water boils; let them have four or five warms; then first pour them into a colander, and then spread a cloth on a table, and put them on that, and dry them well in it: have bottles ready dry'd, and fill them to the necks, and pour over them melted mutton-fat, and cork them down very close, that no air come to them: set them in your cellar, and when you use them, put them into boiling water, with a spoonful of fine sugar, and a good piece of butter: and when they are enough, drain and butter them.

II.--MEAT PIES AND PUDDINGS.

A Battalia Pye:--Take four small chickens, four squab pigeons, four sucking rabbets; cut them in pieces, season them with savoury spice, and lay 'em in the pye, with four sweet-breads sliced, and as many sheep's-tongues, two shiver'd palates, two pair of lamb-stones, twenty or thirty coxcombs, with savoury-balls and oysters. Lay on butter, and close the pye. A lear.

To make an Olio Pye:--Make your pye ready; then take the thin collops of the but-end of a leg of veal; as many as you think will fill your pye; hack them with the back of a knife, and season them with pepper, salt, cloves, and mace; wash over your collops with a bunch of feathers dipped in eggs, and have in readiness a good hand-full of sweet-herbs shred small; the herbs must be thyme, parsley, and spinage; and the yolks of eight hard eggs, minced, and a few oysters parboiled and chopt; some beef-suet shred very fine. Mix these together, and strew them over your collops, and sprinkle a little orange-flower-water on them, and roll the collops up very close, and lay them in your pye, strewing the seasoning that is left over them; put butter on the top, and close up your pye; when 'tis drawn, put in gravy, and one anchovy dissolved in it, and pour it in very hot: and you may put in artichoke-bottoms and chesnuts, if you please, or sliced lemon, or grapes scalded, or what else is in season; but if you will make it a right savoury pye leave them out.

To make a Lumber Pye:--Take a pound and a half of veal, parboil it, and when 'tis cold chop it very small, with two pound of beef-suet, and some candied orange-peel; some sweet-herbs, as thyme, sweet-marjoram, and an handful of spinage; mince the herbs small before you put them to the other; so chop all together, and a pippin or two; then add a handful or two of grated bread, a pound and a half of currants, washed and dried; some cloves, mace, nutmeg, a little salt, sugar and sack, and put to all these as many yolks of raw eggs, and whites of two, as will make it a moist forc'd-meat; work it with your hands into a body, and make it into balls as big as a turkey's egg; then having your coffin made put in your balls. Take the marrow out of three or four bones as whole as you can: let your marrow lie a little in water, to take out the blood and splinters; then dry it, and dip it in yolk of eggs; season it with a little salt, nutmeg grated, and grated bread; lay it on and between your forc'd-meat balls, and over that sliced citron, candied orange and lemon, eryngo-roots, preserved barberries; then lay on sliced lemon, and thin slices of butter over all; then lid your pye, and bake it; and when 'tis drawn, have in readiness a caudle made of white-wine and sugar, and thicken'd with butter and eggs, and pour it hot into your pye.

Very fine Hogs Puddings:--Shred four pounds of beef-suet very fine, mix with it two pounds of fine sugar powder'd, two grated nutmegs, some mace beat, and a little salt, and three pounds of currants wash'd and pick'd; beat twenty-four yolks, twelve whites of eggs, with a little sack; mix all well together, and fill your guts, being clean and steep'd in orange-flower-water; cut your guts quarter and half long, fill them half full; tye at each end, and again thus oooo. Boil them as others, and cut them in balls when sent to the table.

To make Plumb-Porridge:--Take a leg and shin of beef to ten gallons of water, boil it very tender, and when the broth is strong, strain it out, wipe the pot, and put in the broth again; slice six penny-loaves thin, cutting off the top and bottom; put some of the liquor to it, cover it up, and let it stand a quarter of an hour, and then put it in your pot, let it boil a quarter of an hour, then put in five pounds of currants, let them boil a little, and put in five pounds of raisins, and two pounds of prunes, and let them boil till they swell; then put in three quarters of an ounce of mace, half an ounce of cloves, two nutmegs, all of them beat fine, and mix it with a little liquor cold, and put them in a very little while, and take off the pot, and put in three pounds of sugar, a little salt, a quart of sack, and a quart of claret, the juice of two or three lemons; you may thicken with sagoe instead of bread, if you please; pour them into earthen pans, and keep them for use.

III.--SWEET-PUDDINGS, PIES, ETC.

To make New-College Puddings:--Grate a penny stale loaf, and put to it a like quantity of beef-suet finely shred, and a nutmeg grated, a little salt, some currants, and then beat some eggs in a little sack, and some sugar, and mix all together, and knead it as stiff as for manchet, and make it up in the form and size of a turkey-egg, but a little flatter; then take a pound of butter, and put it in a dish, and set the dish over a clear fire in a chafing-dish, and rub your butter about the dish till 'tis melted; put your puddings in, and cover the dish, but often turn your puddings, until they are all brown alike, and when they are enough, scrape sugar over them, and serve them up hot for a side dish.

You must let the paste lie a quarter of an hour before you make up your puddings.

To make a Spread-Eagle pudding:--Cut off the crust of three half-penny rolls, then slice them into your pan; then set three pints of milk over the fire, make it scalding hot, but not boil; so pour it over your bread, and cover it close, and let it stand an hour; then put in a good spoonful of sugar, a very little salt, a nutmeg grated, a pound of suet after 'tis shred, half a pound of currants washed and picked, four spoonfuls of cold milk, ten eggs, but five of the whites; and when all is in, stir it, but not till all is in; then mix it well, butter a dish; less than an hour will bake it.

To make a Cabbage Pudding:--Take two pounds of the lean part of a leg of veal; take of beef-suet the like quantity; chop them together, then beat them together in a stone mortar, adding to it half a little cabbage, scalded, and beat that with your meat; then season it with mace and nutmeg, a little pepper and salt, some green gooseberries, grapes, or barberries in the time of year. In the winter put in a little verjuice; then mix all well together, with the yolks of four or five eggs well beaten; then wrap it up in green cabbage leaves; tye a cloth over it, boil it an hour: melt butter for sauce.

To make a Calf's Foot Pudding:--Take two calf's feet finely shred; then of biskets grated, and stale mackaroons broken small, the quantity of a penny loaf; then add a pound of beef-suet, very finely shred, half a pound of currants, a quarter of a pound of sugar; some cloves, mace and nutmeg, beat fine; a very little salt, some sack and orange-flower-water, some citron and candied orange-peel; work all these well together, with yolks of eggs; if you boil it, put it in the caul of a breast of veal, and tie it over with a cloth; it must boil four hours. For sauce, melt butter, with a little sack and sugar; if you bake it, put some paste in the bottom of the dish, but none on the brim; then melt half a pound of butter, and mix with your stuff, and put it in your dish, and stick lumps of marrow in it; bake it three or four hours; scrape sugar over it, and serve it hot.

To make a Chestnut Pudding:--Take a dozen and half of chestnuts, put them in a skillet of water, and set them on the fire till they will blanch; then blanch them, and when cold, put them in cold water, then stamp them in a mortar, with orange-flower-water and sack, till they are very small; mix them in two quarts of cream, and eighteen yolks of eggs, the whites of three or four; beat the eggs with sack, rose-water and sugar; put it in a dish with puff-paste; stick in some lumps of marrow or fresh butter, and bake it.

To make a Brown-bread Pudding:--Take half a pound of brown bread, and double the weight of it in beef-suet; a quarter of a pint of cream, the blood of a fowl, a whole nutmeg, some cinnamon, a spoonful of sugar, six yolks of eggs, three whites: mix it all well together, and boil it in a wooden dish two hours. Serve it with sack and sugar, and butter melted.

To make a baked Sack Pudding:--Take a pint of cream, and turn it to a curd with a sack; then bruise the curd very small with a spoon; then grate in two Naples-biskets, or the inside of a stale penny-loaf, and mix it well with the curd, and half a nutmeg grated; some fine sugar, and the yolks of four eggs, the whites of two, beaten with two spoonfuls of sack; then melt half a pound of fresh butter, and stir all together till the oven is hot. Butter a dish, and put it in, and sift some sugar over it, just as 'tis going into the oven half an hour will bake it.

To make an Orange Pudding:--Take two large Sevil oranges, and grate off the rind, as far as they are yellow; then put your oranges in fair water, and let them boil till they are tender; shift the water three or four times to take out the bitterness; when they are tender, cut them open, and take away the seeds and strings, and beat the other part in a mortar, with half a pound of sugar, till 'tis a paste; then put in the yolks of six eggs, three or four spoonfuls of thick cream, half a Naples-biscuit grated; mix these together, and melt a pound of very good fresh butter, and stir it well in; when 'tis cold, put a bit of fine puff-paste about the brim and bottom of your dish, and put it in and bake it about three quarters of an hour.

Another sort of Orange Pudding:--Take the outside rind of three Sevil oranges, boil them in several waters till they are tender; then pound them in a mortar with three quarters of a pound of sugar; then blanch and beat half a pound of almonds very fine, with rose-water to keep them from oiling; then beat sixteen eggs, but six whites, and a pound of fresh butter; beat all these together very well till 'tis light and hollow; then put it in a dish, with a sheet of puff-paste at the bottom, and bake it with tarts; scrape sugar on it, and serve it up hot.

To make a French-Barley Pudding:--Take a quart of cream, and put to it six eggs well beaten, but three of the whites; then season it with sugar, nutmeg, a little salt, orange-flower-water, and a pound of melted butter; then put to it six handfuls of French-barley that has been boiled tender in milk: butter a dish, and put it in, and bake it. It must stand as long as a venison-pasty, and it will be good.

To make a Skirret Pye:--Boil your biggest skirrets, and blanch them, and season them with cinamon, nutmeg, and a very little ginger and sugar. Your pye being ready, lay in your skirrets; season also the marrow of three or four bones with cinamon, sugar, a little salt and grated bread. Lay the marrow in your pye, and the yolks of twelve hard eggs cut in halves, a handful of chesnuts boiled and blanched, and some candied orange-peel in slices. Lay butter on the top, and lid your pye. Let your caudle be white-wine, verjuice, some sack and sugar; thicken it with the yolks of eggs, and when the pye is baked, pour it in, and serve it hot. Scrape sugar on it.

To make a Cabbage-Lettuce Pye:--Take some of the largest and hardest cabbage-lettuce you can get; boil them in salt and water till they are tender; then lay them in a colander to drain dry; then have your paste laid in your pattipan ready, and lay butter on the bottom; then lay in your lettuce and some artichoke-bottoms, and some large pieces of marrow, and the yolks of eight hard eggs, and some scalded sorrel; bake it, and when it comes out of the oven, cut open the lid; and pour in a caudle made with white-wine and sugar, and thicken with eggs; so serve it hot.

Potato, or Lemon Cheesecakes:--Take six ounces of potatoes, four ounces of lemon-peel four ounces of sugar, four ounces of butter; boil the lemon-peel til tender, pare and scrape the potatoes, and boil them tender and bruise them; beat the lemon-peel with the sugar, then beat all together very well, and melt all together very well, and let it lie till cold: put crust in your pattipans, and fill them little more than half full: bake them in a quick oven half an hour, sift some double-refined sugar on them as they go into the oven; this quantity will make a dozen small pattipans.

To make Almond Cheesecakes:--Take a good handful or more of almonds, blanch them in warm water, and throw them in cold; pound them fine, and in the pounding put a little sack or orange-flower-water to keep them from oiling; then put to your almonds the yolks of two hard eggs, and beat them together: beat the yolks of six eggs, the whites of three, and mix with your almonds, and half a pound of butter melted, and sugar to your taste; mix all well together, and use it as other cheesecake stuff.

To make the light Wigs:--Take a pound and half of flour, and half a pint of milk made warm; mix these together, and cover it up, and let it lie by the fire half an hour; then take half a pound of sugar, and half a pound of butter; then work these in the paste, and make it into wigs, with as little flour as possible. Let the oven be pretty quick, and they will rise very much.

To make very good Wigs:--Take a quarter of a peck of the finest flour, rub into it three quarters of a pound of fresh butter, till 'tis like grated bread, something more than half a pound of sugar, half a nutmeg, and half a race of ginger grated; three eggs, yolks and whites beaten very well, and put to them half a pint of thick ale-yeast, three or four spoonfuls of sack. Make a hole in your flour, and pour in your yeast and eggs, and as much milk just warm, as will make it into a light paste. Let it stand before the fire to rise half an hour; then make it into a dozen and half of wigs; wash them over with eggs just as they go into the oven; a quick oven, and half an hour will bake them.

To make Carrot or Parsnip Puffs:--Scrape and boil your carrots or parsnips tender; then scrape or mash them very fine, add to a pint of pulp the crumb of a penny-loaf grated, or some stale biscuit, if you have it, some eggs, but four whites, a nutmeg grated, some orange-flower-water, sugar to your taste, a little sack, and mix it up with thick cream. They must be fry'd in rendered suet, the liquor very hot when you put them in; put in a good spoonful in a place.

A Tansy:--Boil a quart of cream or milk with a stick of cinamon, quarter'd nutmeg, and large mace; when half cold, mix it with twenty yolks of eggs, and ten whites; strain it, then put to it four grated biskets, half a pound of butter, a pint of spinage-juice, and a little tansy, sack, and orange-flower-water, sugar, and a little salt; then gather it to a body over the fire, and pour it into your dish, being well butter'd. When it is baked, turn it on a pye-plate; squeeze on it an orange, grate on sugar, and garnish it with slic'd orange and a little tansy. Made in a dish; cut as you please.

To make Sack Cream:--Take the yolks of two eggs, and three spoonfuls of fine sugar, and a quarter of a pint of sack: mix them together, and stir them into a pint of cream; then set them over the fire till 'tis scalding hot, but let it not boil. You may toast some thin slices of white bread, and dip them in sack or orange-flower-water, and pour your cream over them.

To make Quince Cream:--Take quinces, scald them till they are soft; pare them, and mash the clear part of them, and pulp it through a sieve; take an equal weight of quince, and double-refin'd sugar beaten and sifted, and the whites of eggs, and beat it till it is as white as snow, then put it in dishes.

To make Pistachia Cream:--Peel your pistachias, and beat them very fine, and boil them in cream; if 'tis not green enough, add a little juice of spinage; thicken it with eggs, and sweeten to your taste; pour it in basons, and set it by till 'tis cold.

To make white Jelly of Quinces:--Pare your quinces, and cut them in halves; then core them and parboil your quinces; when they are soft, take them up, and crush them through a strainer, but not too hard, only the clear juice. Take the weight of the juice in fine sugar; boil the sugar candy-height, and put in your juice, and let it scald awhile, but not boil; and if any froth arise, scum it off, and when you take it up, have ready a white preserved quince cut in small slices, and lay them in the bottom of your glasses, and pour your jelly to them, it will candy on the top and keep moist on the bottom a long time.

To make Hart's-Horn Jelly:--Take a large gallipot, and fill it full of hart's-horn, and then fill it full with spring-water, and tie a double paper over the gallipot, and set it in the baker's oven with household bread; in the morning take it out, and run it through a jelly-bag, and season it with juice of lemons, and double-refin'd sugar, and the whites of eight eggs well beaten; let it have a boil, and run it thro' the jelly-bag again into your jelly-glasses; put a bit of lemon-peel in the bag.

IV.--CHEESES.

The Queen's Cheese:--Take six quarts of the best stroakings, and let them stand till they are cold; then set two quarts of cream on the fire till 'tis ready to boil; then take it off, and boil a quart of fair water, and take the yolks of two eggs, and one spoonful of sugar, and two spoonfuls of runnet; mingle all these together, and stir it till 'tis blood warm: when the cheese is come, use it as other cheese; set it at night, and the third day lay the leaves of nettles under and over it: it must be turned and wiped, and the nettles shifted every day, and in three weeks it will be fit to eat. This cheese is made between Michaelmas and Alhallontide.

To make a Slip-coat Cheese:--Take new milk and runnet, quite cold, and when 'tis come, break it as little as you can in putting it into the cheese-fat, and let it stand and whey itself for some time; then cover it, and set about two pound weight on it, and when it will hold together, turn it out of that cheese-fat, and keep it turning upon clean cheese-fats for two or three days, till it has done wetting, and then lay it on sharp-pointed dock-leaves till 'tis ripe: shift the leaves often.

To make a New-market Cheese to cut at two Years old:--Any morning in September, take twenty quarts of new milk warm from the cow, and colour it with marigolds: when this is done, and the milk not cold, get ready a quart of cream, and a quart of fair water, which must be kept stirring over the fire till 'tis scalding hot, then stir it well into the milk and runnet, as you do other cheese; when 'tis come, lay cheese-cloths over it, and settle it with your hands; the more hands the better; as the whey rises, take it away, and when 'tis clean gone, put the curd into your fat, breaking it as little as you can; then put it in the press, and press it gently an hour; take it out again, and cut it in thin slices, and lay them singly on a cloth, and wipe them dry; then put it in a tub, and break it with your hands as small as you can, and mix with it a good handful of salt, and a quart of cold cream; put it in the fat, and lay a pound weight on it till next day; then press and order it as others.

V.--CAKES.

To make Shrewsbury Cakes:--Take to one pound of sugar, three pounds of the finest flour, a nutmeg grated, some beaten cinamon; the sugar and spice must be sifted into the flour, and wet it with three eggs, and as much melted butter, as will make it of a good thickness to roll into a paste; mould it well and roll it, and cut it into what shape you please. Perfume them, and prick them before they go into the oven.

To make Whetstone Cakes:--Take half a pound of fine flour, and half a pound of loaf sugar searced, a spoonful of carraway-seeds dried, the yolk of one egg, the whites of three, a little rose-water, with ambergrease dissolved in it; mix it together, and roll it out as thin as a wafer; cut them with a glass; lay them on flour'd paper, and bake them in a slow oven.

To make Portugal Cakes:--Take a pound and a quarter of fine flour well dried, and break a pound of butter into the flour and rub it in, add a pound of loaf-sugar beaten and sifted, a nutmeg grated, four perfumed plums, or some ambergrease; mix these well together, and beat seven eggs, but four whites, with three spoonfuls of orange-flower-water; mix all these together, and beat them up an hour; butter your little pans, and just as they are going into the oven, fill them half full, and searce some fine sugar over them; little more than a quarter of an hour will bake them. You may put a handful of currants into some of them; take them out of the pans as soon as they are drawn, keep them dry, they will keep good three months.

To make Jumbals:--Take the whites of three eggs, beat them well, and take off the froth; then take a little milk, and a little flour, near a pound, as much sugar sifted, a few carraway-seeds beaten very fine; work all these in a very stiff paste, and make them into what form you please bake them on white paper.

To make March-pane:--Take a pound of Jordan almonds, blanch and beat them in a marble mortar very fine; then put to them three-quarters of a pound of double-refin'd sugar, and beat with them a few drops of orange-flower-water; beat all together till 'tis a very good paste, then roll it into what shape you please; dust a little fine sugar under it as you roll it to keep it from sticking. To ice it, searce double-refined sugar as fine as flour, wet it with rose-water, and mix it well together, and with a brush or bunch of feathers spread it over your march-pane: bake them in an oven that is not too hot: put wafer-paper at the bottom, and white paper under that, so keep them for use.

To make the Marlborough Cake:--Take eight eggs, yolks and whites, beat and strain them, and put to them a pound of sugar beaten and sifted; beat it three-quarters of an hour together; then put in three-quarters of a pound of flour well dried, and two ounces of carraway-seeds; beat it all well together, and bake it in a quick oven in broad tin-pans.

To make Wormwood Cakes:--Take one pound of double-refin'd sugar sifted; mix it with the whites of three or four eggs well beat; into this drop as much chymical oil of wormwood as you please. So drop them on paper; you may have some white, and some marble, with specks of colours, with the point of a pin; keep your colours severally in little gallipots. For red, take a dram of cochineel, a little cream of tartar, as much of allum; tye them up severally in little bits of fine cloth, and put them to steep in one glass of water two or three hours. When you use the colour, press the bags in the water, and mix some of it with a little of the white of egg and sugar. Saffron colours yellow; and must be tyed in a cloth, as the red, and put in water. Powder-blue, mix'd with the saffron-water, makes a green; for blue, mix some dry powder-blue with some water.

A French Cake to eat hot:--Take a dozen of eggs, and a quart of cream, and as much flour as will make it into a thick batter; put to it a pound of melted butter, half a pint of sack, one nutmeg grated, mix it well, and let it stand three or four hours; then bake it in a quick oven, and when you take it out, split it in two, and pour a pound of butter on it melted with rose-water; cover it with the other half, and serve it up hot.

To make the thin Dutch Bisket:--Take five pounds of flour, and two ounces of carraway-seeds, half a pound of sugar, and something more than a pint of milk. Warm the milk, and put into it three-quarters of a pound of butter; then make a hole in the middle of your flour, and put in a full pint of good ale-yeast; then pour in the butter and milk, and make these into a paste, and let it stand a quarter of an hour by the fire to rise; then mould it, and roll it into cakes pretty thin; prick them all over pretty much or they will blister; so bake them a quarter of an hour.

To make Dutch Ginger-bread:--Take four pounds of flour, and mix with it two ounces and a half of beaten ginger; then rub in a quarter of a pound of butter, and add to it two ounces of carraway-seeds, two ounces of orange-peel dried and rubb'd to powder, a few coriander-seeds bruised, two eggs: then mix all up in a stiff paste, with two pounds and a quarter of treacle; beat it very well with a rolling-pin, and make it up into thirty cakes; put in a candied citron; prick them with a fork: butter papers three double, one white, and two brown; wash them over with the white of an egg; put them into an oven not too hot, for three-quarters of an hour.

To make Cakes of Flowers:--Boil double-refin'd sugar candy-high, and then strew in your flowers, and let them boil once up; then with your hand lightly strew in a little double-refin'd sugar sifted; and then as quick as may be, put it into your little pans, made of card, and pricked full of holes at bottom. You must set the pans on a pillow, or cushion; when they are cold, take them out.

VI.--CAUDLES AND POSSETS.

To make a Posset with Ale: King-William's Posset:--Take a quart of cream, and mix with it a pint of ale, then beat the yolks of ten eggs, and the whites of four; when they are well beaten, put them to the cream and ale, sweeten it to your taste, and slice some nutmeg in it; set it over the fire, and keep it stirring all the while, and when 'tis thick, and before it boils, take it off, and pour it into the bason you serve it in to the table.

To make the Pope's Posset:--Blanch and beat three-quarters of a pound of al- monds so fine, that they will spread between your fingers like butter, put in water as you beat them to keep them from oiling; then take a pint of sack or sherry, and sweeten it very well with double-refin'd sugar, make it boiling hot, and at the same time put half a pint of water to your almonds, and make them boil; then take both off the fire, and mix them very well together with a spoon; serve it in a china dish.

To make Flummery Caudle:--Take a pint of fine oatmeal, and put to it two quarts of fair water: let it stand all night, in the morning stir it, and strain it into a skillet, with three or four blades of mace, and a nutmeg quartered; set it on the fire, and keep it stirring, and let it boil a quarter of an hour; if it is too thick, put in more water, and let it boil longer; then add a pint of Rhenish or white-wine; three spoon- fuls of orange-flower-water, the juice of two lemons and one orange, a bit of butter, and as much fine sugar as will sweeten it; let all these have a warm, and thicken it with the yolks of two or three eggs. Drink it hot for a breakfast.

To make Tea Caudle:--Make a quart of strong green tea, and pour it out into a skillet, and set it over the fire; then beat the yolks of four eggs and mix with them a pint of white-wine, a grated nutmeg, sugar to your taste, and put all together; stir it over the fire till 'tis very hot, then drink it in china dishes as caudle.

VII.--CONSERVES, DRIED AND CAN-DIED FRUITS, MARMALADES, ETC.

To dry Apricocks like Prunella's:--Take a pound of Apricocks; being cut in halves or quarters, let them boil till they be very tender in a thin syrup; let them stand a day or two in the stove, then take them out of the syrup, and lay them drying till they be as dry as prunello's, then box them: you may make your syrup red with the juice of red plums; if you please you may pare them.

To candy Angelica:--Take angelica that is young, and cut it in fit lengths, and boil it till it is pretty tender, keeping it close covered; then take it up and peel off all the strings; then put it in again, and let it simmer and scald till 'tis very green; then take it up and dry it in a cloth, and weigh it, and to every pound of angelica take a pound of double-refin'd sugar beaten and sifted; put your angelica in an earthen pan, and strew the sugar over it, and let it stand two days; then boil it till it looks very clear, put it in a colander to drain the syrup from it, and take a little double-refin'd sugar and boil it to sugar again; then throw in your angelica, and take it out in a little time, and put it on glass plates. It will dry in your stove, or in an oven after pyes are drawn.

To candy Orange-Flowers:--Take half a pound of double-refin'd sugar finely beaten, wet it with orange-flower-water, then boil it candy-high, then put in a handful of orange-flowers, keeping it stirring, but let it not boil, and when the sugar candies about them, take it off the fire, drop it on a plate, and set it by till 'tis cold.

To make Conserve of Red-Roses, or any other Flowers:--Take rose-buds, and pick them, and cut off the white part from the red, and put the red flowers, and sift them through a sieve to take out the seeds; then weigh them, and to every pound of flowers take two pounds and a half of loaf-sugar, beat the flowers pretty fine in a stone mortar; then by degrees put the sugar to them, and beat it very well till 'tis well incorporated together; then put it into gallipots, and tye it over with paper, and over that leather, and it will keep seven years.

To preserve white Pear Plumbs:--Take pear plumbs when they are yellow, before they are too ripe; give them a slit in the seam, and prick them behind; make your water almost scalding hot, and put a little sugar to it to sweeten it, and put in your plumbs and cover them close; set them on the fire to coddle, and take them off sometimes a little, and set them on again: take care they do not break; have in readiness as much double-refin'd sugar boiled to a height as will cover them, and when they are coddled pretty tender, take them out of that liquor, and put them into your preserving-pan to your syrup, which must be but blood-warm when your plumbs go in. Let them boil till they are clear, scum them and take them off, and let them stand two hours; then set them on again and boil them, and when they are thoroughly preserved, take them up and lay them in glasses; boil your syrup till 'tis thick; and when 'tis cold, put in your plumbs; and a month after, if your syrup grows thin, you must boil it again, or make a fine jelly of pippins, and put on them. This way you may do the pimordian plumb, or any white plumb, and when they are cold, paper them up.

To preserve Mulberries whole:--Set some mulberries over the fire in a skillet, and draw from them a pint of juice, when 'tis strained. Then take three pounds of sugar, beaten very fine; wet the sugar with the pint of juice; boil up your sugar, and scum it, and put in two pounds of ripe mulberries, and let them stand in the syrup till they are thoroughly warm; then set them on the fire, and let them boil very gently; do them but half enough, so put them by in the syrup till next day; then boil them gently again, and when the syrup is pretty thick, and will stand in a round drop when 'tis cold, they are enough; so put all together in a gallipot for use.

To preserve whole Quinces white:--Take the largest quinces of the greenest colour, and scald them till they are pretty soft; then pare them and core them with a scoop; then weigh your quinces against so much double-refin'd sugar, and make a syrup of one half, and put in your quinces, and boil them as fast as you can; then you must have in readiness pippin liquor; let it be very strong of the pippins, and when 'tis strained out, put in the other half of your sugar, and make it a jelly, and when your quinces are clear, put them into the jelly, and let them simmer a little; they will be very white; so glass them up, and when they are cold, paper them and keep them in a stove.

To make white Quince Marmalade:--Scald your quinces tender, take off the skin and pulp them from the core very fine, and to every pound of quince have a pound and half of double-refin'd sugar in lumps, and half a pint of water; dip your sugar in the water and boil and scum it till 'tis a thick syrup: then put in your quince, boil and scum it on a quick fire a quarter of an hour, so put it in your pots.

To make red Quince Marmalade:--Pare and core a pound of quince, beat the parings and cores and some of your worst quinces, and strain out the juice; and to every pound of quince take ten or twelve spoonfuls of that juice, and three-quarters of a pound of loaf-sugar; put all into your preserving-pan, cover it close, and let it stew over a gentle fire two hours; when 'tis of an orange-red, uncover and boil it up as fast as you can: when of a good colour, break it as you like it, give it a boil, and pot it up.

To make Melon Mangoes:--Take small melons, not quite ripe, cut a slip down the side, and take out the inside very clean; beat mustard-seeds, and shred garlick, and mix with the seeds, and put in your mangoes; put the pieces you cut out into their places again, and tye them up, and put them into your pot, and boil some vinegar (as much as you think will cover them) with whole pepper, and some salt, and Jamaica pepper, and pour in scalding hot over your mangoes, and cover them close to keep in the steam; and so do every day for nine times together, and when they are cold cover them with leather.

To make Conserve of Hips:--Gather the hips before they grow soft, cut off the heads and stalks, slit them in halves, and take out all the seed and white that is in them very clean; then put them in an earthen pan, and stir them every day, else they will grow mouldy; let them stand till they are soft enough to rub through a coarse hair-sieve; as the pulp comes, take it off the sieve; they are a dry berry, and will require pains to rub it through; then add its weight in sugar, and mix it well together without boiling; keeping it in deep gallipots for use.

To make clear Cakes of Gooseberries:--Take your white Dutch gooseberries when they are thorough ripe, break them with your fingers and squeeze out all the pulp into a fine piece of cambrick or thick muslin to run thro' clear; then weigh the juice and sugar one against the other; then boil the juice a little while, then put in your sugar and let it dissolve, but not boil; scum it and put it into glasses, and stove it in a warm stove.

To make white Quince Paste:--Scald the quinces tender to the core, and pare them, and scrape the pulp clean from the core, beat it in a mortar, and pulp it through a colander; take to a pound of pulp a pound and two ounces of sugar, boil the sugar till 'tis candy-high; then put in your pulp, stir it about constantly till you see it come clear from the bottom of the preserving-pan; then take it off, and lay it on plates pretty thin: you may cut it in what shape you please, or make quince chips of it; you must dust it with sugar when you put it into the stove, and turn it on papers in a sieve, and dust the other side; when they are dry, put them in boxes with papers between. You may make red quince paste the same way as this, only colour the quince with cochineel.

To make Syrup of any flower:--Clip your flowers, and take their weight in sugar; then take a high gallipot, and a row of flowers, and a strewing of sugar, till the pot is full; then put in two or three spoonfuls of the same syrup or still'd water; tye a cloth on the top of the pot, and put a tile on that, and set your gallipot in a kettle of water over a gentle fire, and let it infuse till the strength is out of the flowers, which will be in four or five hours; then strain it thro' a flannel, and when 'tis cold bottle it up.

VIII.--PICKLES.

To pickle Nasturtium-Buds:--Gather your little knobs quickly after your blossoms are off; put them in cold water and salt for three days, shifting them once a day; then make a pickle (but do not boil it at all) of some white-wine, some white-wine vinegar, eschalot, horse-radish, pepper, salt, cloves, and mace whole, and nutmeg quartered; then put in your seeds and stop them close; they are to be eaten as capers.

To keep Quinces in Pickle:--Cut five or six quinces all to pieces, and put them in an earthen pot or pan, with a gallon of water and two pounds of honey; mix all these together well, and then put them in a kettle to boil leisurely half an hour, and then strain your liquor into that earthen pot, and when 'tis cold, wipe your quinces clean, and put them into it: they must be covered very close, and they will keep all the year.

To pickle Ashen-keys:--Take ashen-keys as young as you can get them, and put them in a pot with salt and water; then take green whey, when 'tis hot, and pour over them; let them stand till they are cold before you cover them, so let them stand; when you use them, boil them in fair water; when they are tender take them out, and put them in salt and water.

To pickle Pods of Radishes:--Gather the youngest pods, and put them in water and salt twenty-four hours; then make a pickle for them of vinegar, cloves, mace, whole pepper: boil this, and drain the pods from the salt and water, and pour the liquor on them boiling hot: put to them a clove of garlick a little bruised.

To pickle Broom-Buds:--Put your broom-buds into little linnen-bags, tie them up, and make a pickle of bay-salt and water boiled, and strong enough to bear an egg; put your bags in a pot, and when your pickle is cold, put it to them; keep them close, and let them lie till they turn black; then shift them two or three times, till they change green; then take them out, and boil them as you have occasion for them: when they are boiled, put them out of the bag: in vinegar they will keep a month after they are boiled.

To pickle Purslain Stalks:--Wash your stalks, and cut them in pieces six inches long; boil them in water and salt a dozen walms; take them up, drain them, and when they cool, make a pickle of stale beer, white-wine vinegar, and salt, put them in, and cover them close.

IX.--WINES.

To make strong Mead:--Take of spring-water what quantity you please, and make it more than blood-warm, and dissolve honey in it till 'tis strong enough to bear an egg, the breadth of a shilling; then boil it gently near an hour, taking off the scum as it rises; then put to about nine or ten gallons, seven or eight large blades of mace, three nutmegs quarter'd, twenty cloves, three or four sticks of cinamon, two or three roots of ginger, and a quarter of an ounce of Jamaica pepper; put these spices into the kettle to the honey and water, a whole lemon, with a sprig of sweet-briar, and a sprig of rosemary; tie the briar and rosemary together, and when they have boiled a little while, take them out and throw them away; but let your liquor stand on the spice in a clean earthen pot till the next day; then strain it into a vessel that is fit for it; put the spice in a bag, and hang it in the vessel, stop it, and at three months draw it into bottles. Be sure that 'tis fine when 'tis bottled; after 'tis bottled six weeks 'tis fit to drink.

To make small White Mead:--Take three gallons of spring-water and make it hot, and dissolve in it three quarts of honey and a pound of loaf sugar; and let it boil about half an hour, and scum it as long as any rises, then pour it out into a tub, and squeeze in the juice of four lemons; put in the rinds of but two; twenty cloves, two races of ginger, a top of sweet-briar, and a top of rosemary. Let it stand in a tub till 'tis but blood warm; then make a brown toast and spread it with two or three spoonfuls of ale-yeast, put it into a vessel fit for it; let it stand four or five days, then bottle it out.

To make Frontiniac Wine:--Take six gallons of water and twelve pounds of white sugar, and six pounds of raisins of the sun cut small; boil these together an hour; then take of the flowers of elder, when they are falling and will shake off, the quantity of half a peck; put them in the liquor when 'tis almost cold, the next day put in six spoonfuls of syrup of lemons, and four spoonfuls of ale-yeast, and two days after put it in a vessel that is fit for it, and when it has stood two months bottle it off.

To make English Champagne, or the fine Currant Wine:--Take to three gallons of water nine pounds of Lisbon sugar; boil the water and sugar half an hour, scum it clean, then have one gallon of currants pick'd, but not bruised, pour the liquor boiling-hot over them, and when cold, work it with half a pint of balm two days; then pour it through a flannel or sieve, then put it into a barrel fit for it with half an ounce of ising-glass well bruised; when it has done working, stop it close for a month, then bottle it, and in every bottle put a very small lump of double-refin'd sugar. This is excellent wine, and has a beautiful colour.

To make Saragossa Wine, or English Sack:--To every quart of water, put a sprig of rue, and to every gallon a handful of fennel-roots, boil these half an hour, then strain it out, and to every gallon of this liquor put three pounds of honey; boil it two hours, and scum it well, and when 'tis cold pour it off and turn it into a vessel, or such cask that is fit for it; keep it a year in the vessel, and then bottle it; 'tis a very good sack.

Mountain Wine:--Pick out the big stalks of your Malaga raisins, then chop them very small, five gallons to every gallon of cold spring-water, let them steep a fortnight or more, squeeze out the liquor and barrel it in a vessel fit for it; first fume the vessel with brimstone; don't stop it up till the hissing is over.

To make Quince Wine;--Take your quinces when they are thorough ripe, wipe off the fur very clean; then take out the cores and bruise them as you do apples for cyder, and press them, and to every gallon of juice put two pounds and a half of fine sugar, stir it together till 'tis dissolved; then put it in your cask, and when it has done working stop it close; let it stand till March before you bottle it. You may keep it two or three years, it will be better.

To make Plumb Wine:--Take twenty pounds of Malaga raisins, pick, rub, and shred them, and put them into a tub; then take four gallons of fair water and boil it an hour, and let it stand till 'tis blood-warm; then put it to your raisins; let it stand nine or ten days, stirring it once or twice a day, strain out your liquor, and mix with it two quarts of damson juice, put it in a vessel, and when it has done working, stop it close; at four or five months bottle it.

To make Birch Wine:--In March bore a hole in a tree, and put in a faucet, and it will run two or three days together without hurting the tree; then put in a pin to stop it, and the next year you may draw as much from the same hole; put to every gallon of the liquor a quart of good honey, and stir it well together, boil it an hour, scum it well, and put in a few cloves, and a piece of lemon-peel; when 'tis almost cold, put to it so much ale-yeast as will make it work like new ale, and when the yeast begins to settle, put it in a runlet that will just hold it: so let it stand six weeks or longer if you please; then bottle it, and in a month you may drink it. It will keep a year or two. You may make it with sugar, two pounds to a gallon, or something more, if you keep it long. This is admirably wholesome as well as pleasant, an opener of obstructions, good against the phthisick, and good against the spleen and scurvy, a remedy for the stone, it will abate heat in a fever or thrush, and has been given with good success.

To make Sage Wine:--Boil twenty-six quarts of spring-water a quarter of an hour, and when 'tis blood-warm, put twenty-five pounds of Malaga raisins pick'd, rubb'd and shred into it, with almost half a bushel of red sage shred, and a porringer of ale-yeast; stir all well together, and let it stand m a tub cover'd warm six or seven days, stirring it once a day; then strain it out, and put it in a runlet. Let it work three or four days, stop it up; when it has stood six or seven days put in a quart or two of Malaga sack, and when 'tis fine bottle it.

Sage Wine another way:--Take thirty pounds of Malaga raisins pick'd clean, and shred small, and one bushel of green sage shred small, then boil five gallons of water, let the water stand till 'tis luke-warm; then put it in a tub to your sage and raisins; let it stand five or six days, stirring it twice or thrice a day; then strain and press the liquor from the ingredients, put it in a cask, and let it stand six months: then draw it clean off into another vessel; bottle it in two days; in a month or six weeks it will be fit to drink, but best when 'tis a year old.

To make Ebulum:--To a hogshead of strong ale, take a heap'd bushel of elder-berries, and half a pound of juniper-berries beaten; put in all the berries when you put in the hops, and let them boil together till the berries brake in pieces, then work it up as you do ale; when it has done working, add to it half a pound of ginger, half an ounce of cloves, as much mace, an ounce of nutmegs, and as much cinamon grosly beaten, half a pound of citron, as much eringo-root, and likewise of candied orange-peel; let the sweetmeats be cut in pieces very thin, and put with the spice into a bag and hang it in the vessel when you stop it up. So let it stand till 'tis fine, then bottle it up and drink it with lumps of double-refined sugar in the glass.

To make Cock Ale:--Take ten gallons of ale, and a large cock, the older the better, parboil the cock, flea him, and stamp him in a stone mortar till his bones are broken, (you must craw and gut him when you flea him) put the cock into two quarts of sack, and put to it three pounds of raisins of the sun stoned, some blades of mace, and a few cloves; put all these into a canvas bag, and a little before you find the ale has done working, put the ale and bag together into a vessel; in a week or nine days' time bottle it up, fill the bottles but just above the necks, and leave the same time to ripen as other ale.

To make it Elder Ale:--Take ten bushels of malt to a hogshead, then put two bushels of elder-berries pickt from the stalks into a pot or earthen pan, and set it in a pot of boiling water till the berries swell, then strain it out and put the juice into the guile-fat, and beat it often in, and so order it as the common way of brewing.

To clear Wine:--Take half a pound of hartshorn, and dissolve it in cyder, if it be for cyder, or Rhenish-wine for any liquor: this is enough for a hogshead.

To fine Wine the Lisbon way:--To every twenty gallons of wine take the whites of ten eggs, and a small handful of salt, beat it together to a froth, and mix it well with a quart or more of the wine, then pour it in the vessel, and in a few days it will be fine.

COOKERY BOOKS.
PART III.

In 1747 appeared a thin folio volume, of which I will transcribe the title: "The Art of Cookery, Made Plain and Easy, which far Exceeds Every Thing of the Kind Ever yet Published ... By a Lady. London: Printed for the Author; and sold at Mrs. Ashburn's, a China Shop, the Corner of Fleet Ditch. MDCCXLVII." The lady was no other than Mrs. Glasse, wife of an attorney residing in Carey Street; and a very sensible lady she was, and a very sensible and interesting book hers is, with a preface showing that her aim was to put matters as plainly as she could, her intention being to instruct the lower sort. "For example," says she, "when I bid them lard a fowl, if I should bid them lard with large lardoons they would not know what I meant; but when I say they must lard with little pieces of Bacon, they know what I mean." I have been greatly charmed with Hannah Glasse's "Art of Cookery," 1747, and with her "Complete Confectioner" likewise in a modified degree. The latter was partly derived, she tells you, from the manuscript of "a very old experienced housekeeper to a family of the first distinction." But, nevertheless, both are very admirable performances; and yet the compiler survives scarcely more than in an anecdote for which I can see no authority. For she does not say, "First catch your hare"[3].

Mrs. Glasse represents that, before she undertook the preparation of the volume on confectionery, there was nothing of the kind for reference and consultation. But we had already a curious work by E. Kidder, who was, according to his title-page, a teacher of the art which he expounded eventually in print. The title is sufficiently descriptive: "E. Kidder's Receipts of Pastry and Cookery, for the use of his Scholars,

---

3   Mrs. Glasse's cookery book was reprinted at least as late as 1824

who teaches at his School in Queen Street, near St. Thomas Apostle's[4], on Mondays, Tuesdays and Wednesdays, in the afternoon. Also on Thursdays, Fridays and Saturdays, in the afternoon, at his School next to Furnivalls Inn in Holborn. Ladies may be taught at their own Houses." It is a large octavo, consisting of fifty pages of engraved text, and is embellished with a likeness of Mr. Kidder. For all that Mrs. Glasse ignores him.

I have shown how Mrs. Glasse might have almost failed to keep a place in the public recollection, had it not been for a remark which that lady did not make. But there is a still more singular circumstance connected with her and her book, and it is this--that in Dr. Johnson's day, and possibly in her own lifetime, a story was current that the book was really written by Dr. Hill the physician. That gentleman's claim to the authorship has not, of course, been established, but at a dinner at Dilly's the publisher's in 1778, when Johnson, Miss Seward, and others were present, a curious little discussion arose on the subject. Boswell thus relates the incident and the conversation:--"The subject of cookery having been very naturally introduced at a table, where Johnson, who boasted of the niceness of his palate, avowed that 'he always found a good dinner,' he said, 'I could write a better book about cookery than has ever yet been written; it should be a book upon philosophical principles. Pharmacy is now made much more simple. Cookery may be so too. A prescription, which is now compounded of five ingredients, had formerly fifty in it. So in Cookery. If the nature of the ingredients is well known, much fewer will do. Then, as you cannot make bad meat good, I would tell what is the best butcher's meat, the best beef, the best pieces; how to choose young fowls; the proper seasons of different vegetables; and then how to roast, and boil, and compound."

DILLY:--"Mrs. Glasse's 'Cookery,' which is the best, was written by Dr. Hill. Half the trade know this."

JOHNSON:--"Well, Sir, that shews how much better the subject of cookery may be treated by a philosopher. I doubt if the book be written by Dr Hill; for in Mrs. Glasse's Cookery, which I have looked into, saltpetre and salt-prunella are spoken of as different substances, whereas salt-prunella is only saltpetre burnt on charcoal; and Hill could not be ignorant of this. However, as the greatest part of such a book is made by transcription, this mistake may have been carelessly adopted. But

---

4 In another edition his school is in St. Martin's Le Grand

you shall see what a book of cookery I could make. I shall agree with Mr. Dilly for the copyright."

Miss SEWARD:--"That would be Hercules with the distaff indeed!"

JOHNSON:--"No, Madam. Women can spin very well; but they cannot make a good book of cookery."

But the Doctor's philosophical cookery book belongs to the voluminous calendar of works which never passed beyond the stage of proposal; he did not, so far as we know, ever draw out a title-page, as Coleridge was fond of doing; and perhaps the loss is to be borne with. The Doctor would have pitched his discourse in too high a key.

Among the gastronomical enlargements of our literature in the latter half of the last century, one of the best books in point of classification and range is that by B. Clermont, of which the third edition made its appearance in 1776, the first having been anonymous. Clermont states that he had been clerk of the kitchen in some of the first families of the kingdom, and lately to the Earl of Abingdon. But elsewhere we find that he had lived very recently in the establishment of the Earl of Ashburnham, for he observes in the preface: "I beg the candour of the Public will excuse the incorrectness of the Language and Diction. My situation in life as an actual servant to the Earl of Ashburnham at the time of the first publication of this Book will I trust plead my Apology." He informs his readers on the title-page, and repeats in the preface, that a material part of the work consists of a translation of "Les Soupers de la Cour," and he proceeds to say, that he does not pretend to make any further apology for the title of *supper*, than that the French were, in general, more elegant in their suppers than their dinners. In other words, the late dinner was still called supper.

The writer had procured the French treatise from Paris for his own use, and had found it of much service to him in his capacity as clerk of the kitchen, and he had consequently translated it, under the persuasion that it would prove an assistance to gentlemen, ladies, and others interested in such matters. He specifies three antecedent publications in France, of which his pages might be considered the essence, viz., "La Cuisine Royale," "Le Maitre d'Hotel Cuisinier," and "Les Dons de Comus"; and he expresses to some of his contemporaries, who had helped him in his researches, his obligations in the following terms:--"As every country produces many Articles peculiar to itself, and considering the Difference of Climates, which either forward or retard them, I would not rely on my own Knowledge, in regard to such Articles; I applied therefore to three Tradesmen, all eminent in their Profession, one for Fish, one for Poultry, and one for the productions of the Garden, viz., Mr. Humphrey Turner, the Manager in St. James's Market; Mr. Andrews, Poulterer in ditto; and Mr. Adam Lawson, many years chief gardener to the Earl of Ashburnham; in this article I was also assisted by Mr. Rice, Green-Grocer, in St. Albans Street." Clermont dates his remarks from Princes Street, Cavendish Square.

While Mrs. Glasse was still in the middle firmament of public favour, a little book without the writer's name was published as by "A Lady." I have not seen the first or second editions; but the third appeared in 1808. It is called "A New System of Domestic Cookery, Formed upon Principles of Economy, and Adapted to the use of Private Families." The author was Helene Rundell, of whom I am unable to supply any further particulars at present. Mrs. Rundell's cookery book, according to the preface, was originally intended for the private instruction of the daughters of the authoress in their married homes, and specially prepared with an eye to housekeepers of moderate incomes. Mrs. Rundell did not write for professed cooks, or with any idea of emolument; and she declared that had such a work existed when she first set out in life it would have been a great treasure to her. The public shared the writer's estimate of her labours, and called for a succession of impressions of the "New System," till its run was checked by Miss Acton's still more practical collection. Mrs. Rundell is little consulted nowadays; but time was when Mrs. Glasse and herself were the twin stars of the culinary empyrean.

Coming down to our own times, the names most familiar to our ears are Ude, Francatelli, and Soyer, and they are the names of foreigners[5]. No English school of cookery can be said ever to have existed in England. We have, and have always had, ample material for making excellent dishes; but if we desire to turn it to proper ac-

---

5 A fourth work before me has no clue to the author, but it is like the others, of an alien complexion. It is called "French Domestic Cookery, Combining Elegance and Economy. In twelve Hundred Receipts, 12mo, 1846." Soyer's book appeared in the same year. In 1820, an anonymous writer printed a Latin poem of his own composition, called "Tabella Cibaria, a Bill of Fare, etc., etc., with Copious Notes," which seem more important than the text

count, we have to summon men from a distance to our aid, or to accept the probable alternative--failure. The adage, "God sends meat, and the devil sends cooks," must surely be of native parentage, for of no country is it so true as of our own. Perhaps, had it not been for the influx among us of French and Italian experts, commencing with our Anglo-Gallic relations under the Plantagenets, and the palmy days of the monastic orders, culinary science would not have arrived at the height of development which it has attained in the face of great obstacles. Perchance we should not have progressed much beyond the pancake and oatmeal period. But foreign *chefs* limit their efforts to those who can afford to pay them for their services. The middle classes do not fall within the pale of their beneficence. The poor know them not. So it happens that even as I write, the greater part of the community not only cannot afford professional assistance in the preparation of their meals, which goes without saying, but from ignorance expend on their larder twice as much as a Parisian or an Italian in the same rank of life, with a very indifferent result. There are handbooks of instruction, it is true, both for the middle and for the lower classes. These books are at everybody's command. But they are either left unread, or if read, they are not understood. I have before me the eleventh edition of Esther Copley's "Cottage Comforts," 1834; it embraces all the points which demand attention from such as desire to render a humble home comfortable and happy. The leaves have never been opened. I will not say, ex hoc disce omnes; but it really appears to be the case, that these works are not studied by those for whom they are written--not studied, at all events, to advantage.

Dr. Kitchener augmented this department of our literary stores in 1821 with his "Cook's Oracle," which was very successful, and passed through a series of editions.

In the preface to that of 1831, the editor describes the book as greatly enlarged and improved, and claims the "rapid and steady sale which has invariably attended each following edition" as a proof of the excellence of the work. I merely mention this, because in Kitchener's own preface to the seventh issue, 12mo, 1823, he says: "This last time I have found little to add, and little to alter." Such is human fallibility!

The "Cook's Oracle" was heralded by an introduction which very few men could have written, and which represents the Doctor's method of letting us know that, if we fancy him an impostor, we are much mistaken. "The following Recipes," says he, "are not a mere marrowless collection of shreds and patches, of cuttings and pastings--but a bona-fide register of practical facts--accumulated by a perseverance, not to be subdued or evaporated by the igniferous Terrors of a Roasting Fire in the Dog-days:--in defiance of the odoriferous and calefaceous repellents of Roasting, Boiling,--Frying, and Broiling;--moreover, the author has submitted to a labour no preceding Cookery-Book-maker, perhaps, ever attempted to encounter,--having eaten each Receipt before he set it down in his Book."

What could critics say, after this? One or two large editions must have been exhausted before they recovered their breath, and could discover how the learned Kitchener set down the receipts which he had previously devoured. But the language of the Preface helps to console us for the loss of Johnson's threatened undertaking in this direction.

Dr. Kitchener proceeded on different lines from an artist who closely followed him in the order of publication; and the two did not probably clash in the slightest degree. The cooking world was large enough to hold Kitchener and the ci-devant chef to the most Christian King Louis XVI. and the Right Honourable the Earl of Sefton, Louis Eustache Ude. Ude was steward to the United Service Club, when he printed his "French Cook" in 1822. A very satisfactory and amusing account of this volume occurs in the "London Magazine" for January 1825. But whatever may be thought of Ude nowadays, he not only exerted considerable influence on the higher cookery of his day, but may almost be said to have been the founder of the modern French school in England.

Ude became *chef* at Crockford's Club, which was built in 1827, the year in which his former employer, the Duke of York, died. There is a story that, on hearing of the Duke's illness, Ude exclaimed, "Ah, mon pauvre Duc, how much you shall miss me where you are gone!"

About 1827, Mrs. Johnstone brought out her well-known contribution to this section of literature under the title of "The Cook and Housewife's Manual," veiling her authorship under the pseudonym of Mistress Margaret Dods, the landlady in Scott's tale of "St. Ronan's Well," which appeared three years before (8vo, 1824).

Mrs. Johnstone imparted a novel feature to her book by investing it with a fictitious history and origin, which, like most inventions of the kind, is scarcely consistent with the circumstances, however it may tend to enliven the monotony of a professional publication.

After three prefaces in the fourth edition before me (8vo, 1829) we arrive at a heading, "Institution of the Cleikum Club," which narrates how Peregrine Touchwood, Esquire, sought to cure his *ennui* and hypochondria by studying Apician mysteries; and it concludes with the syllabus of a series of thirteen lectures on cookery, which were to be delivered by the said Esquire. One then enters on the undertaking itself, which can be readily distinguished from an ordinary manual by a certain literary tone, which certainly betrays a little the hand or influence of Scott.

But though the present is a Scottish production, there is no narrow specialism in its scheme. The title-page gives a London publisher as well as an Anglo-Athenian one, and Mrs. Johnstone benevolently adapted her labours to her countrywomen and the unworthier Southrons alike.

I imagine, however, that of all the latter-day master-cooks, Alexis Soyer is most remembered. His "Gastronomic Regenerator," a large and handsome octavo volume of between 700 and 800 pages, published in 1846, lies before me. It has portraits of the compiler and his wife, and many other illustrations, and is dedicated to a Royal Duke. It was produced under the most influential patronage and pressure, for Soyer was overwhelmed with engagements, and had scruples against appearance in print. He tells us that in some library, to which he gained access, he once found among the works of Shakespeare and other *chefs* in a different department, a volume with the words "Nineteenth Edition" upon it, and when he opened it, he saw to his great horror "A receipt for Ox-tail Soup!" Why this revelation exercised such a terrifying effect he proceeds to explain. It was the incongruity of a cookery book in the temple of the Muses. But nevertheless, such is the frailty of our nature, that he gradually, on regaining his composure, and at such leisure intervals as he could command, prepared the "Gastronomic Regenerator," in which he eschewed all superfluous ornaments of diction, and studied a simplicity of style germane to the subject; perchance he had looked into Kitchener's Preface. He lets us know that he had made collections of the same kind at an earlier period of his career, but had destroyed them, partly owing to his arduous duties at the Reform Club, and partly to the depressing influence of the nineteenth edition of somebody else's cookery book--probably, by the way, Ude's. The present work occupied some ten months, and was prepared amid the most stupendous interruptions from fair visitors to the Club (15,000), dinners for the members and their friends (25,000), dinner parties of importance (38), and the meals for the staff (60). He gives a total of 70,000 dishes; but it is not entirely clear whether these refer to the 38 dinner parties of importance, or to the 25,000 of inferior note, or to both. The feeling of dismay at the nineteenth edition of somebody must have been sincere, for he winds up his preface with an adjuration to his readers (whom, in the "Directions for Carving," he does not style Gentle, or Learned, or Worshipful, but HONOURABLE) not to place his labours on the same shelf with "Paradise Lost."

Soyer had also perhaps certain misgivings touching too close an approximation to other ***chefs*** besides Milton and Shakespeare, for he refers to the "profound ideas" of Locke, to which he was introduced, to his vast discomfort, "in a most superb library in the midst of a splendid baronial hall." But the library of the Reform Club probably contained all this heterogeneous learning. Does the "Gastronomic Regenerator," out of respect to the fastidious sentiments of its author, occupy a separate apartment in that institution with a separate curator?

It seems only the other day to me, that Soyer took Gore Lodge, and seemed in a fair way to make his removal from the Reform Club a prosperous venture. But he lost his wife, and was unfortunate in other ways, and the end was very sad indeed. "Soyez tranquille," was the epitaph proposed at the time by some unsentimental wagforpoor Madame Soyer; it soon served for them both.

But nearly concurrent with Soyer's book appeared one of humble pretensions, yet remarkable for its lucidity and precision, Eliza Acton's "Modern Cookery in all its Branches reduced to an easy practice," 16mo, 1845. I have heard this little volume highly commended by competent judges as exactly what it professes to be; and the quantities in the receipts are particularly reliable.

The first essay to bring into favourable notice the produce of Colonial cattle was, so far as I can collect, a volume published in 1872, and called "Receipts for Cooking Australian Meat, with Directions for preparing Sauces suitable for the same." This still remains a vexed question; but the consumption of the meat is undoubtedly on the increase, and will continue to be, till the population of Australasia equalises supply and demand.

COOKERY BOOKS.
PART IV.

Besides the authorities for this branch of the inquiry already cited, there are a few others, which it may assist the student to set down herewith:--

1. A Collection of Ordinances and Regulations for the Government of the Royal Household (Edward III. to William and Mary). 4to, 1790.

2. The book of Nurture. By Hugh Rhodes, of the King's Chapel. Printed in the time of Henry VIII. by John Redman. 4to.

3. A Breviate touching the Order and Government of the House of a Nobleman. 1605. *Archaeologia*, xiii.

4. Orders made by Henry, Prince of Wales, respecting his Household. 1610. *Archaeologia*, xiv.

5. The School of Good Manners. By William Phiston or Fiston. 8vo, 1609.

6. The School of Virtue, the Second Part. By Richard West. 12mo, 1619.

7. The School of Grace; or, A Book of Nurture. By John Hart. 12mo. (About 1680.)

8. England's Newest Way in all Sorts of Cookery. By Henry Howard, Free Cook of London. 8vo, London, 1703.

9. A Collection of above three hundred Receipts in Cookery, Physick and Surgery, for the use of all Good Wives, Tender Mothers, and Careful Nurses. By several Hands. The second edition, to which is added a second part. 8vo, London, 1729. Fifth edition, 8vo, London, 1734.

10. The Compleat City and Country Cook. By Charles Carter. 8vo, London, 1732.

11. The Compleat Housewife: or, Accomplish'd Gentlewomans Companion: Being a collection of upwards of Five Hundred of the most approved Receipts in

Cookery, Pastry, Confectionery, Preserving, Pickles, Cakes, Creams, Jellies, Made Wines, Cordials. With Copper Plates.... And also Bills of Fare for every month in the year.... By E. Smith. Seventh edition, with very large additions, near fifty Receipts being communicated just before the author's death. 8vo, London, 1736. Eleventh edition. 8vo, London, 1742.

12. The Complete Family Piece: A very Choice Collection of Receipts in... Cookery. Seventh Edition. 8vo, London, 1737.

13. The Modern Cook. By Vincent La Chapelle, cook to the Prince of Orange. Third edition. 8vo, London, 1744.

14. A Treatise of all Sorts of Foods, both Animal and Vegetable, and also of Drinkables, written originally in French by the Learned M.L. Lemery. Translated by D. Hay, M.D. 8vo, London, 1745.

15. The Housekeeper's Pocket-Book. By Sarah Harrison. Sixth edition, 2 vols. 12mo, London, 1755.

16. Professed Cookery. By Ann Cook. Third edition. 8vo, London (about 1760).

17. The Experienced English Housekeeper. By Elizabeth Raffald. Second edition. 8vo, London, 1771. There were an eighth, tenth, and eleventh editions, and two others, described as "New Editions," between this date and 1806. The compiler dedicates her book to "The honourable Lady Elizabeth Warburton," in whose service she had been. She mentions that the volume was published by subscription, and that she had obtained eight hundred names. In the preface Mrs. Raffald begins by observing: "When I reflect upon the number of books already in print upon this subject, and with what contempt they are read, I cannot but be apprehensive that this may meet the same fate with some who will censure before they either see it or try its value." She concludes by saying that she had not meddled with physical receipts, "leaving them to the physician's superior judgment, whose proper province they are." The author of the "Experienced Housekeeper" tells us that she had not only filled that post in noble families during fifteen years, but had travelled with her employers, and so widened her sphere of observation.

18. The Young Ladies' Guide in the Art of Cookery. By Elizabeth Marshall. 8vo, Newcastle, 1777.

19. English Housewifery Exhibited in above 450 Receipts. By Elizabeth Moxon.

Fourth edition. 8vo, Leeds (about 1780).

20. The Practice of Modern Cookery. By George Dalrymple. 8vo, Edinburgh, 1781.

21. The Ladies' Assistant for Regulating and Supplying the Table. By Charlotte Mason. 8vo, London, 1786.

22. The Compleat Family Companion. 8vo, London, 1787 (?).

23. The Honours of the Table; or, Rules for Behaviour during Meals, with the whole Art of Carving.... By the Author of "Principles of Politeness," etc. (Trusler). Second edition. Woodcuts by Bewick. 12mo, London, 1791.

24. The French Family Cook: being a complete system of French Cookery. From the French. 8vo, London, 1793.

25. The British Housewife; or, The Cook's, Housekeeper's, and Gardener's Companion. By Martha Bradley. 8vo.

26. Cookery and Pastry. By Mrs. Macivey. New edition, 12mo, Edinburgh, 1800.

27. The London Art of Cookery. By John Farley. Fourth edition. 8vo, London, 1807.

28. The School of Good Living; or, A Literary and Historical Essay on the European Kitchen, beginning with Cadmus, the Cook and King, and concluding with the Union of Cookery and Chymistry. 12 mo, London, 1804.

29. Culina Famulatur Medicina. Receipts in Modern Cookery, with a Medical Commentary by Ignotus, and revised by A. Hunter, M.D., F.A.S.L. and E. Fourth edition, 12mo, York, 1806.

30. The Universal Cook. By Francis Collingwood and T. Woollams. Fourth edition. 8vo, London, 1806.

31. A Complete System of Cookery. By John Simpson, Cook. 8vo, London, 1806. Again, 8vo, London, 1816.

32. Simpson's Cookery Improved and Modernised. By H.W. Brand. 8vo, London, 1834.

33. The Imperial and Royal Cook. By Frederick Nutt, Esquire, Author of the "Complete Confectioner." 8vo, London, 1809.

34. The Housekeeper's Domestic Library. By Charles Millington. 8vo, London, 1810.

35. The Housekeeper's Instructor; or, Universal Family Book. By W.A. Henderson. Seventeenth edition. By S.C. Schrubbelie, Cook to the Albany, London. 8vo, London, 1811.

36. The Art of Preserving all kinds of animal and vegetable Substances for several years. By M. Appert. Translated from the French. Second edition. 8vo, London, 1812. With a folding Plate.

37. Domestic Economy and Cookery, for Rich and Poor. By a Lady. 8vo, London, 1827. In the preface the author apprises us that a long residence abroad had enabled her to become a mistress of the details of foreign European cookery; but she adds: "The mulakatanies and curries of India; the sweet pillaus, yahourt, and cold soups of Persia; the cubbubs, sweet yaughs and sherbets of Egypt; the cold soups and mixed meats of Russia, the cuscussous and honeyed paste of Africa, have been inserted with the view of introducing a less expensive and more wholesome and a more delicate mode of cookery."

38. Apician Morsels; or, Tales of the Table, Kitchen, and Larder. By Dick Humelbergius Secundus. 8vo, London, 1834.

39. Cottage Economy and Cookery. 8vo, London, 1844[6].

DIET OF THE YEOMAN AND THE POOR.

The staple food among the lower orders in Anglo-Saxon and the immediately succeeding times was doubtless bread, butter, and cheese, the aliment which goes so far even yet to support our rural population, with vegetables and fruit, and occasional allowances of salted bacon and pancakes, beef, or fish. The meat was usually boiled in a kettle suspended on a tripod[7] over a wood-fire, such as is used only now, in an improved shape, for fish and soup.

The kettle which is mentioned, as we observe, in the tale of "Tom Thumb," was the universal vessel for boiling purposes[8], and the bacon-house (or larder), so called from the preponderance of that sort of store over the rest, was the warehouse

---

6 Reprinted from the Journal of the Agricultural Society, 1843, vol. iii, part I

7 The tripod is still employed in many parts of the country for a similar purpose

8 An inverted kettle was the earliest type of the diving-bell

for the winter stock of provisions[9]. The fondness for condiments, especially garlic and pepper, among the higher orders, possibly served to render the coarser nourishment of the poor more savoury and flavorous. "It is interesting to remark," says Mr. Wright[10], "that the articles just mentioned (bread, butter, and cheese) have preserved their Anglo-Saxon names to the present time, while all kinds of meat--beef, veal, mutton, pork, even bacon--have retained only the names given to them by the Normans; which seems to imply that flesh-meat was not in general use for food among the lower classes of society."

In Malory's compilation on the adventures of King Arthur and his knights, contemporary with the "Book of St. Alban's," we are expressly informed in the sixth chapter, how the King made a great feast at Caerleon in Wales; but we are left in ignorance of its character. The chief importance of details in this case would have been the excessive probability that Malory would have described an entertainment consonant with the usage of his own day, although at no period of early history was there ever so large an assemblage of guests at one time as met, according to the fable, to do honour to Arthur.

In the tenth century Colloquy of Archbishop Alfric, the boy is made to say that he is too young to eat meat, but subsists on cabbages, eggs, fish, cheese, butter, beans, and other things, according to circumstances; so that a vegetable diet was perhaps commoner in those days even among the middle classes than at present. This youth, when he is asked what he drinks, replies, water, or ale if he can get it. The dish so deftly constructed by King Arthur, according to one of his numerous biographers, exhibited that wedlock of fruit with animal matter--fat and plums--which we post-Arthurians eye with a certain fastidious repugnance, but which, notwithstanding, lingered on to the Elizabethan or Jacobaean era--nay, did not make the gorge of our grandsires turn rebellious. It survives among ourselves only in the modified shape of such accessories as currant jelly and apple sauce.

But the nursery rhyme about Arthur and the bag-pudding of barley meal with raisins and meat has a documentary worth for us beyond the shadowy recital of

---

9 What is called in some places the keeping-room also accommodated flitches on the walls, and hams ranged along the beams overhead; and it served at the same time for a best parlour

10 "Domestic Manners and Sentiments," 1862, p. 91

the banquet at Caerleon, for, mutato nomine, it is the description of a favourite article of popular diet in the fifteenth and sixteenth centuries. The narrative of Mrs. Thumb and her pudding is more circumstantial than that of King Alfred and the housewife; and if the tradition is worthless, it serves us so far, that it faithfully portrays a favourite item of rustic consumption in old times. We are told that the pudding was made in a bowl, and that it was chiefly composed of the flesh and blood of a newly-killed hog, laid in batter; and then, when all was ready, the bag with all its savoury burden was put into a kettle.

As we are already on the threshold of legend and myth, we may linger there a moment to recall to memory the resemblance between the description of this piece of handiwork and that ascribed to good King Arthur, who lived in days when monarchs were their own *chefs*, for the Arthurian dish was also prepared in a bag, and consisted, according to the ditty, of barley-meal and fat. Soberly speaking, the two accounts belong, maybe, to something like the same epoch in the annals of gastronomy; and a large pudding was, for a vast length of time, no doubt, a prevailing piece de resistance in all frugal British households. It was the culinary forefather of toad-in-the-hole, hot-pot, Irish stew, and of that devil-dreaded Cornish pasty. The Elizabethan transmitters of these two Apician nuggets possibly antedated the popular institution of the bag-pudding; but the ancientest gastronomical records testify to the happy introduction of the frying-pan about the era when we were under Alfred's fatherly sway. It may have even preceded the grill, just as the fork lagged behind the spoon, from which it is a seeming evolution. That no reader may doubt the fact, that Tom's mother made the pudding, and that Tom held the candle, we refer to the old edition of this choice piece of chapman's ware, where an accurate drawing of Mrs. Thumb, and the board, and the bowl, and Tom with the candle, may be inspected. The prima stamina of the modern fruit-pudding really appear to be found in the ancient bag-pudding, of which Tom Thumb had such excellent reason to be acquainted with the contents. The mode of construction was similar, and both were boiled in a cloth. The material and subsidiary treatment of course differed; but it is curious that no other country possesses either the tart or the pudding, as we understand them, and as the latter has perhaps been developed from the dish, of the making of which Tom Thumb was an eye-witness to his sorrow, so the covered fruit tart may not improbably be an outgrowth from the old coffin pasty of venison or game, with the superaddition of a dish for the safe custody of the juice.

Another rather prominent factor in the diet of the poor classes, not only in Scotland but in the North of England, was oatmeal variously prepared. One very favourable and palatable way was by grinding the meal a second time as fine as flour, boiling it, and then serving it with hot milk or treacle. There is something in the nature of this food so peculiarly satisfying and supporting, that it seems to have been destined to become the staple nourishment of a poor population in a cold and bracing climate. The fourteenth and fifteenth centuries unquestionably saw a great advance in the mystery of cookery and in the diversity of dishes, and the author of "Piers of Fulham" complains, that men were no longer satisfied with brawn and powdered beef, which he terms "store of house," but would have venison, wild fowl, and heronshaw; and men of simple estate, says he, will have partridges and plovers, when lords lack. He adds quaintly:

> "A mallard of the dunghill is good enough for me,
>   With pleasant pickle, or it is else poison. pardy."

We have for our purpose a very serviceable relic of the old time, called "A Merry Jest, how the Ploughman learned his Paternoster." The scene purports to be laid in France, and the general outline may have been taken from the French; but it is substantially English, with allusions to Kent, Robin Hood, and so forth, and it certainly illustrates the theme upon which we are. This ploughman was in fact a farmer or husbandman, and the account of his dwelling and garden-stuff is very interesting. We are told that his hall-roof was full of bacon-flitches, and his store-room of eggs, butter, and cheese. He had plenty of malt to make good ale--

> "And Martlemas beef to him was not dainty; Onions
> and Garlic had he enough,
>   And good cream, and milk of the cow."

But in "Vox Populi Vox Dei," written about 1547, and therefore apparently not from the pen of Skelton, who died in 1529, it is said that the price of an ox had risen to four pounds, and a sheep without the wool to twelve shillings and upwards, so that the poor man could seldom afford to have meat at his table. This evil the writer ascribes to the exactions of the landlord and the lawyer. The former charged too highly for his pastures, and the latter probably advanced money on terms. The old poem depicts in sad colours the condition of the yeoman at the same period, that had had once plenty of cows and cream, butter, eggs, cheese, and honey; all which had gone to enrich upstarts who throve by casting-counters and their pens. The story of the "King and a poor Northern Man," 1640, also turns upon the tyranny of the lawyers over ignorant clients.

The "Serving-man's Comfort," 1598, draws a somewhat gloomy picture of the times. The prices of all provisions, among other points, had trebled since the good old days, when his father and grandfather kept house. Then people could buy an ox for 20s., a sheep for 3s., a calf for 2s., a goose for 6d., a capon for 4d., a hen for 2d., a pig for the same, and all other household provisions at a like rate. The reason given by the farmer was that the landlords had raised their rent. Let them have the land on the old terms, and the former prices would pay. This plea and demand have come back home to us in 1886.

The tradition is, that when Queen Elizabeth received the intelligence of the defeat of the Armada, she was dining off a goose--doubtless about eleven o'clock in the morning. It was an anxious moment, and perhaps her majesty for the moment had thrown ceremony somewhat aside, and was "keeping secret house."

The author of the "Serving-man's Comfort," 1598, also laments the decay of hospitality. "Where," he inquires "are the great chines of stalled beef, the great, black jacks of double beer, the long hall-tables fully furnished with good victuals?" But he seems to have been a stickler for the solid fare most in vogue, according to his complaint, formerly; and he represents to us that in lieu of it one had to put up with goose-giblets, pigs' pettitoes, and so many other boiled meats, forced meats, and made dishes. Things were hardly so very bad, however, if, as he states previously, the curtailment of the expenditure on the table still left, as a medium repast, two or three dishes, with fruit and cheese after. The black jack here mentioned was not discarded till comparatively modern days. Nares, who published his Glossary in 1822, states that he recollects them in use.

"A meal's meat twice a week, worth a groat," is mentioned as the farm servant's portion in "Civil and Uncivil Life," 1579. In "A Piece of Friar Bacon's Brasen-heads

Prophesie," a unique poem, 1604, we read that at that time a cheesecake and a pie were held "good country meat." The author adds:

"Ale and Spice, and Curdes and Creame,   Would make a Scholler make a Theame."

Breton, in his "Fantasticks," 1626, observes: "Milk, Butter and Cheese are the labourers dyet; and a pot of good Beer quickens his spirits."

Norfolk dumplings were celebrated in John Day the playwright's time. He has put into the mouth of his east-country yeoman's son, Tom Strowd, in "The Blind Beggar of Bethnal Green," written long before it was printed in 1659, the following:--"As God mend me, and ere thou com'st into Norfolk, I'll give thee as good a dish of Norfolk dumplings as ere thou laydst thy lips to;" and in another passage of the same drama, where Swash's shirt has been stolen, while he is in bed, he describes himself "as naked as your Norfolk dumplin." In the play just quoted, Old Strowd, a Norfolk yeoman, speaks of his contentment with good beef, Norfolk bread, and country home-brewed drink; and in the "City Madam," 1658, Holdfast tells us that before his master got an estate, "his family fed on roots and livers, and necks of beef on Sundays." I cite these as traits of the kind of table kept by the lower grades of English society in the seventeenth century.

MEATS AND DRINKS.

Slender: You are afraid, if you see the bear loose, are you not?

Anne: Aye, indeed, Sir

Slender: That's meat and drink to me, now.

MERRY WIVES OF WINDSOR, i, 1.

The manufacture of wine and of fruit preserves, and many of the processes of cookery, could have scarcely been accomplished without a large and constant supply of sugar.

The exact date of the first introduction of the latter into England continues to be a matter of uncertainty. It was clearly very scarce, and doubtless equally dear, when, in 1226, Henry III. asked the Mayor of Winchester to procure him three pounds of Alexandria sugar, if so much could be got, and also some rose and violet-coloured sugar; nor had it apparently grown much more plentiful when the same prince ordered the sheriffs of London to send him four loaves of sugar to Woodstock. But it soon made its way into the English homes, and before the end of the thirteenth century it could be procured even in remote provincial towns. It was sold either by the loaf or the pound. It was still exorbitantly high in price, varying from eighteen pence to three shillings a pound of coeval currency; and it was retailed by the spice-dealers.

In Russell's "Book of Nurture," composed about 1450, it occurs as an ingredient in hippocras; and one collects from a letter sent by Sir Edward Wotton to Lord Cobham from Calais in 1546, that at that time the quantities imported were larger, and the price reduced; for Wotton advises his correspondent of a consignment of five-and-twenty loaves at six shillings the loaf. One loaf was equal to ten pounds; this brought the commodity down to eight pence a pound of fifteenth century money.

The sugar of Cyprus was also highly esteemed; that of Bezi, in the Straits of Sunda, was the most plentiful; but the West Indian produce, as well as that of Mauritius, Madeira, and other cane-growing countries, was unknown.

Of bread, the fifteenth century had several descriptions in use: pain-main or bread of very fine flour, wheat-bread, barley-meal bread, bran-bread, bean-bread, pease-bread, oat-bread or oat-cakes, hard-bread, and unleavened bread. The poor often used a mixture of rye, lentils, and oatmeal, varied according to the season and district.

The author of "The Serving-man's Comfort," 1598, however, seems to say that it was counted by the poorer sort at that time a hardship only to be tolerated in a dear year to mix beans and peas with their corn, and he adds: "So must I yield you a loaf of coarse cockle, having no acquaintance with coin to buy corn."

In a ***Nominale*** of this period mention is made of "oblys," or small round loaves, perhaps like the old-fashioned "turnover"; and we come across the explicit phrase, a loaf of bread, for the first time, a pictorial vocabulary of the period even furnishing us with a representation of its usual form.

Nor were the good folks of those days without their simnels, cracknels, and other sorts of cakes for the table, among which in the ***wastel*** we recognise the equivalent of the modern French ***gateau***.

Besides march-pain or pain-main, and pain-puff, two sorts baked on special occasions, and rather entering into the class of confectionery, our better-to-do ancestors usually employed three descriptions of bread: manchete for the master's table, made of fine boulted flour; chete, of unboulted flour, but not mixed with any coarser ingredient; and brown-bread, composed of flour and rye meal, and known as **maslin** (mystelon).

A bushel of wheat, in a romance of the thirteenth century, is estimated to produce twenty loaves; but the statement is obviously to be taken with allowance. The manchet was sometimes thought to be sufficient without butter, as we now eat a scone. In the "Conceits of Old Hobson," 1607, the worthy haberdasher of the Poultry gives some friends what is facetiously described as a "light" banquet--a cup of wine and a manchet of bread on a trencher for each guest, in an apartment illuminated with five hundred candles.

There is no pictorial record of the mode in which the early baker worked here, analogous to that which Lacroix supplies of his sixteenth century **confrere**. The latter is brought vividly enough before us in a copy of one of Jost Amman's engravings, and we perceive the bakery and its tenants: one (apparently a female) kneading the dough in a trough at the farther end, a second by a roasting fire, with a long ladle or peel in his hand, putting the loaf on the oven, and a third, who is a woman, leaving the place with two baskets of bread, one on her head and one on her arm; the baker himself is almost naked, like the operatives in a modern iron furnace. The artist has skilfully realised the oppressive and enervating atmosphere; and it was till lately quite usual to see in the side streets of Paris in the early morning the **boulanger** at work precisely in the same informal costume. So tenacious is usage, and so unchanging many of the conditions of life.

The Anglo-Norman used butter where his Italian contemporary used oil. But it is doubtful whether before the Conquest our ancestors were commonly acquainted with butter.

The early cook understood the art of glazing with yolk of egg, and termed it endoring, and not less well that of presenting dishes under names calculated to mislead the intended partaker, as where we find a receipt given for pome de oringe, which turns out to be a preparation of liver of pork with herbs and condiments, served up in the form of glazed force-meat balls.

Venison was salted in troughs. In the tale of "The King and the Hermit," the latter exhibits to his unknown visitor his stock of preserved venison from the deer, which he had shot in the forest.

The mushroom, of which so many varieties are at present recognised by botanists, seems, from the testimony of an Italian, Giacomo Castelvetri, who was in London in 1614, and to whom I have already referred, to have been scarcely known here at that time. I cannot say, of course, how far Castelvetri may have prosecuted his inquiries, though he certainly leaves the impression of having been intelligently observant; or whether he includes in this observation the edible toadstools; but even now much unreasonable prejudice exists as to the latter, and very limited use is made of any but two or three familiar sorts of the mushroom itself. It is a pity that this misconception should not be dissipated.

Caviary had been brought into England, probably from Russia, at the commencement of the seventeenth century, perhaps sooner. In 1618, "The Court and Country," by Breton, seems to represent it as an article of diet which was little known, and not much relished; for a great lady had sent the writer's father a little barrel of it, and it was no sooner opened than it was fastened down again, to be returned to the donor with a respectful message that her servant had black soap enough already.

In the time of James I. the ancient bill of fare had been shorn of many of its coarser features, so far as fish was concerned; and the author of "The Court and Country" tells a story to shew that porpoise-pie was a dish which not even a dog would eat.

The times had indeed changed, since a King and a Cardinal-archbishop judged this warm-blooded sea-dweller a fit dish for the most select company.

It is not a despicable or very ascetic regimen which Stevenson lays before us under April in his reproduction of Breton's "Fantasticks," 1626, under the title of the "Twelve Months," 1661:--"The wholesome dyet that breeds good sanguine juyce, such as pullets, capons, sucking veal, beef not above three years Old, a draught of morning milk fasting from the cow; grapes, raysons, and figs be good before meat; Rice with Almond Milk, birds of the Field, Peasants and Partridges, and fishes of stony rivers, Hen eggs potcht, and such like."

Under May he furnishes us with a second and not less appetising *menu*:--

"Butter and sage are now the wholesome Breakfast, but fresh cheese and cream are meat for a dainty mouth; the early Peascods and Strawberries want no price with great Bellies; but the Chicken and the Duck are fatted for the Market; the sucking Rabbet is frequently taken in the Nest, and many a Gosling never lives to be a Goose."

Even so late as the succeeding reign, Breton speaks of the good cheer at Christmas, and of the cook, if he lacks not wit, sweetly licking his fingers.

The storage of liquids became a difficult problem where, as among our ancestors, glazed pottery was long unknown; and more especially with regard to the supply of water in dry seasons. But so far as milk was concerned, the daily yield probably seldom exceeded the consumption; and among the inhabitants further north and east, who, as Caesar says, partook also of flesh, and did not sow grain--in other words, were less vegetarian in their habits from the more exhausting nature of the climate--the consideration might be less urgent. It is open to doubt if, even in those primitive times, the supply of a national want lagged far behind the demand.

The list of wines which the King of Hungary proposed to have at the wedding of his daughter, in "The Squire of Low Degree," is worth consulting. Harrison, in his "Description of England," 1586, speaks of thirty different kinds of superior vintages and fifty-six of commoner or weaker kinds. But the same wine was perhaps known under more than one name.

Romney or Rumney, a Hungarian growth, Malmsey from the Peloponnesus, and Hippocras were favourites, and the last-named was kept as late as the last century in the buttery of St. John's College, Cambridge, for use during the Christmas festivities. But France, Spain, Greece, almost all countries, contributed to furnish the ancient wine-cellar, and gratify the variety of taste among connoisseurs; and for such as had not the means to purchase foreign productions, the juice of the English grape, either alone or mingled with honey and spice, furnished a not unpalatable and not very potent stimulant. As claret and hock with us, so anciently Bastard and Piment were understood in a generic sense, the former for any mixed wine, the latter for one seasoned with spice.

In "Colin Blobol's Testament," a whimsical production of the fifteenth century, Tent and Valencia wines are mentioned, with wine of Languedoc and Orleans. But perhaps it will be best to cite the passage:--

"I trow there shall be an honest fellowship, save first shall they of ale have new backbones. With strong ale brewed in vats and in tuns; Ping, Drangollie, and the Draget fine, Mead, Mattebru, and the Metheling. Red wine, the claret and the white, with Tent and Alicant, in whom I delight. Wine of Languedoc and of Orleans thereto: Single beer, and other that is double: Spruce beer, and the beer of Hamburgh: Malmsey, Tires, and Romany."

But some of the varieties are hidden under obscure names. We recognise Muscadel, Rhine wine, Bastard, Hippocras, however. On the 10th of December, 1497, Piers Barber received six shillings and eight pence, according to the "Privy Purse Expences of Henry VII.," "for spice for ypocras."

Metheglin and beer of some kind appear to be the most ancient liquors of which there are any vestiges among the Britons. Ferguson, in his Essay "On the Formation of the Palate," states that they are described by a Greek traveller, who visited the south of Britain in the fourth century B.C. This informant describes metheglin as composed of wheat and honey (of course mixed with water), and the beer as being of sufficient strength to injure the nerves and cause head-ache.

Worlidge, in his "Vinetum Britannicum," 1676, gives us receipts for metheglin and birch wine. Breton, in his "Fantasticks," 1626, under January, recommends a draught of ale and wormwood wine mixed in a morning to comfort the heart, scour the maw, and fulfil other beneficial offices.

The English beer of by-gone times underwent many vicissitudes, and it was long before our ancestors conquered their dislike to the bitter hop, after having been accustomed to a thick, sweet liquor of which the modern Kentish ale is in some measure a survival. Beer was made from a variety of grain; oats were most commonly employed. In France, they resorted even to vetches, lentils, rye, and darnel. But as a rule it was a poor, thin drink which resulted from the operation, and the monks of Glastonbury deemed themselves fortunate in being allowed by their abbot to put a load of oats into the vat to improve the quality of the beverage; which may account for Peter of Blois characterising the ale in use at Court in his day (he died about the end of the twelfth century) as potent--it was by contrast so. The first assize of ale seems not to have been enacted till the reign of Henry III.

From a glossary of the fourteenth century, inserted in "Reliquse Antique," 1841, it appears that whey was then used as a drink; it occurs there as "cerum, i, quidam liquor, whey."

THE KITCHEN.

In direct connection with cookery as with horticulture, are the utensils and appliances which were at the command of those who had to do with these matters in days of yore; and in both cases an inquirer finds that he has to turn from the vain search for actual specimens belonging to remoter antiquity to casual representations or descriptions in MSS. and printed books. Our own museums appear to be very weakly furnished with examples of the vessels and implements in common use for culinary purposes in ancient times, and, judging from the comparatively limited information which we get upon this subject from the pages of Lacroix, the paucity of material is not confined to ourselves. The destruction and disappearance of such humble monuments of the civilisation of the past are easily explained; and the survival of a slender salvage is to be treated as a circumstance not less remarkable than fortunate.

It seems that the practice was to cut up, if not to slaughter, the animals used for food in the kitchen, and to prepare the whole carcase, some parts in one way and some in another. We incidentally collect from an ancient tale that the hearts of swine were much prized as dainties.

Besides a general notion of the appointments of the cooking department, we are enabled to form some conception of the aspect of the early kitchen itself from extant representations in the "Archaeological Album," the "Penny Magazine" for 1836, and Lacroix[11]. The last-named authority furnishes us with two interesting sixteenth century interiors from Jost Amman, and (from the same source) a portraiture of the cook of that period.

The costume of the subject is not only exhibited, doubtless with the fidelity characteristic of the artist, but is quite equally applicable to France, if not to our own country, and likewise to a much earlier date. The evidences of the same class supplied by the "Archaeological Album," 1845, are drawn from the MS. in the British Museum, formerly belonging to the Abbey of St. Albans. They consist of two illustrations--one of Master Robert, cook to the abbey, as elsewhere noticed, ac-

---

11 "Moeurs, Usages et Costumes au Moyen Age," 1872, pp 166, 170, 177

companied by his wife--unique relic of its kind; the other a view of a small apartment with dressers and shelves, and with plates and accessories hung round, in which a cook, perhaps the identical Master Robert aforesaid, is plucking a bird. The fireplace is in the background, and the iron vessel which is to receive the fowl, or whatever it may really be, is suspended over the flame by a long chain. The perspective is rather faulty, and the details are not very copious; but for so early a period as the thirteenth or early part of the following century its value is undeniable.

The "Penny Magazine" presents us with a remarkable exterior, that of the venerable kitchen of Stanton-Harcourt, near Oxford, twenty-nine feet square and sixty feet in height. There are two large fireplaces, facing each other, but no chimney, the smoke issuing atthe holes, each about seven inches in diameter, which run round the roof. As Lamb said of his Essays, that they were all Preface, so this kitchen is all chimney. It is stated that the kitchen at Glastonbury Abbey was constructed on the same model; and both are probably older than the reign of Henry IV. The one to which I am more immediately referring, though, at the time (1835) the drawing was taken, in an excellent state of preservation, had evidently undergone repairs and structural changes.

It was at Stanton-Harcourt that Pope wrote a portion of his translation of Homer, about 1718.

A manufactory of brass cooking utensils was established at Wandsworth in or before Aubrey's time by Dutchmen, who kept the art secret. Lysons states that the place where the industry was carried on bore the name of the "Frying Pan Houses"[12].

In the North of England, the ***bake-stone***, originally of the material to which it owed its name, but at a very early date constructed of iron, with the old appellations retained as usual, was the universal machinery for baking, and was placed on the ***Branderi***, an iron frame which was fixed on the top of the fireplace, and consisted of iron bars, with a sliding or slott bar, to shift according to the circumstances.

The tripod which held the cooking-vessel over the wood flame, among the former inhabitants of Britain, has not been entirely effaced. It is yet to be seen here and there in out-of-the-way corners and places; and in India they use one con-

12 A "Environs of London," 1st ed., Surrey, pp. 502-3

structed of clay, and differently contrived. The most primitive pots for setting over the fire on the tripod were probably of bronze.

The tripod seems to be substantially identical with what was known in Nidderdale as the kail-pot. "This was formerly in common use," says Mr. Lucas; "a round iron pan, about ten inches deep and eighteen inches across, with a tight-fitting, convex lid. It was provided with three legs. The kail-pot, as it was called, was used for cooking pies, and was buried bodily in burning peat. As the lower peats became red-hot, they drew them from underneath, and placed them on the top. The kail-pot may still be seen on a few farms." This was about 1870.

The writer is doubtless correct in supposing that this utensil was originally employed for cooking kail or cabbage and other green stuff.

Three rods of iron or hard wood lashed together, with a hook for taking the handle of the kettle, formed, no doubt, the original tripod. But among some of the tribes of the North of Europe, and in certain Tartar, Indian, and other communities, we see no such rudimentary substitute for a grate, but merely two uprights and a horizontal rest, supporting a chain; and in the illustration to the thirteenth or fourteenth century MS., once part of the abbatial library at St. Albans, a nearer approach to the modern jack is apparent in the suspension of the vessel over the flame by a chain attached to the centre of a fireplace.

Not the tripod, therefore, but the other type must be thought to have been the germ of the later-day apparatus, which yielded in its turn to the Range.

The fireplace with a ring in the middle, from which is suspended the pot, is represented in a French sculpture of the end of the fourteenth century, where two women are seated on either side, engaged in conversation. One holds a ladle, and the other an implement which may be meant for a pair of bellows.

In his treatise on Kitchen Utensils, Neckam commences with naming a table, on which the cook may cut up green stuff of various sorts, as onions, peas, beans, lentils, and pulse; and he proceeds to enumerate the tools and implements which are required to carry on the work: pots, tripods for the kettle, trenchers, pestles, mortars, hatchets, hooks, saucepans, cauldrons, pails, gridirons, knives, and so on. The head-cook was to have a little apartment, where he could prepare condiments and dressings; and a sink was to be provided for the viscera and other offal of poultry. Fish was cooked in salt water or diluted wine.

Pepper and salt were freely used, and the former must have been ground as it was wanted, for a pepper-mill is named as a requisite. Mustard we do not encounter till the time of Johannes de Garlandia (early thirteenth century), who states that it grew in his own garden at Paris. Garlic, or gar-leac (in the same way as the onion is called **yn-leac**), had established itself as a flavouring medium. The nasturtium was also taken into service in the tenth or eleventh century for the same purpose, and is classed with herbs.

When the dish was ready, it was served up with green sauce, in which the chief ingredients were sage, parsley, pepper, and oil, with a little salt. Green geese were eaten with raisin or crab-apple sauce. Poultry was to be well larded or basted while it was before the fire.

I may be allowed to refer the reader, for some interesting jottings respecting the first introduction of coal into London, to "Our English Home," 1861. "The middle classes," says the anonymous writer, "were the first to appreciate its value; but the nobility, whose mansions were in the pleasant suburbs of Holborn and the Strand, regarded it as a nuisance." This was about the middle of the thirteenth century. It may be a mite contributed to our knowledge of early household economy to mention, by the way, that in the supernatural tale of the "Smith and his Dame" (sixteenth century) "a quarter of coal" occurs. The smith lays it on the fire all at once; but then it was for his forge. He also poured water on the flames, to make them, by means of his bellows, blaze more fiercely. But the proportion of coal to wood was long probably very small. One of the tenants of the Abbey of Peterborough, in 852, was obliged to furnish forty loads of wood, but of coal two only.

In the time of Charles I., however, coals seem to have been usual in the kitchen, for Breton, in this "Fantasticks," 1626, says, under January:--"The Maid is stirring betimes, and slipping on her Shooes and her Petticoat, groaps for the tinder box, where after a conflict between the steele and the stone, she begets a spark, at last the Candle lights on his Match; then upon an old rotten foundation of broaken boards she erects an artificiall fabrick of the black Bowels of New-Castle soyle, to which she sets fire with as much confidence as the Romans to their Funerall Pyles."

Under July, in the same work, we hear of "a chafing dish of coals;" and under September, wood and coals are mentioned together. But doubtless the employment of the latter was far less general.

In a paper read before the Royal Society, June 9, 1796, there is an account of a saucepan discovered in the bed of the river Withain, near Tattersall Ferry, in Lincolnshire, in 1788. It was of base metal, and was grooved at the bottom, to allow the contents more readily to come within reach of the fire. The writer of this narrative, which is printed in the "Philosophical Transactions," considered that the vessel might be of Roman workman-ship; as he states that on the handle was stamped a name, C. ARAT., which he interprets Caius Aratus. "It appears," he adds, "to have been tinned; but almost all the coating had been worn off.... The art of tinning copper was understood and practised by the Romans, although it is commonly supposed to be a modern invention."

Neckam mentions the roasting-spit, elsewhere called the roasting-iron; but I fail to detect skewers, though they can hardly have been wanting. Ladles for basting and stirring were familiar. As to the spit itself, it became a showy article of plate, when the fashion arose of serving up the meat upon it in the hall; and the tenure by which Finchingfield in Essex was held in capite in the reign of Edward III.--that of turning the spit at the coronation--demonstrates that the instrument was of sufficient standing to be taken into service as a memorial formality.

The fifteenth century vocabulary notices the salt-cellar, the spoon, the trencher, and the table-cloth. The catalogue comprises morsus, a bit, which shows that *bit* and *bite* are synonymous, or rather, that the latter is the true word as still used in Scotland, Yorkshire, and Lincolnshire, from the last of which the Pilgrims carried it across the Atlantic, where it is a current Americanism, not for one bite, but as many as you please, which is, in fact, the modern provincial interpretation of the phrase, but not the antique English one. The word *towel* was indifferently applied, perhaps, for a cloth for use at the table or in the lavatory. Yet there was also the *manuturgium*, or hand-cloth, a speciality rendered imperative by the mediaeval fashion of eating.

In the inventory of the linen at Gilling, in Yorkshire, one of the seats of the Fairfax family, made in 1590, occur:--"Item, napkins vj. dozen. Item, new napkins vj. dozen." This entry may or may not warrant a conclusion that the family bought that quantity at a time--not a very excessive store, considering the untidy habits of eating and the difficulty of making new purchases at short notice.

Another mark of refinement is the resort to the *napron*, corruptly *apron*, to protect the dress during the performance of kitchen work. But the fifteenth century was evidently growing wealthier in its articles of use and luxury; the garden and the kitchen only kept pace with the bed-chamber and the dining-hall, the dairy and the laundry, the stable and the out-buildings. An extensive nomenclature was steadily growing up, and the Latin, old French, and Saxon terms were giving way on all sides to the English. It has been now for some time an allowed and understood thing that in these domestic backgrounds the growth of our country and the minuter traits of private life are to be studied with most clear and usurious profit.

The trencher, at first of bread, then of wood, after a while of pewter, and eventually of pottery, porcelain or china-earth, as it was called, and the precious metals, afforded abundant scope for the fancy of the artist, even in the remote days when the material for it came from the timber-dealer, and sets of twelve were sometimes decorated on the face with subjects taken from real life, and on the back with emblems of the purpose to which they were destined.

Puttenham, whose "Art of English Poetry" lay in MS. some years before it was published in 1589, speaks of the posies on trenchers and banqueting dishes. The author of "Our English Home" alludes to a very curious set, painted in subjects and belonging to the reign of James I., which was exhibited at the Society of Antiquaries' rooms by Colonel Sykes.

It is to be augured that, with the progress of refinement, the meats were served upon the table on dishes instead of trenchers, and that the latter were reserved for use by the guests of the family. For in the "Serving-man's Comfort," 1598, one reads:--"Even so the gentlemanly serving-man, whose life and manners doth equal his birth and bringing up, scorneth the society of these sots, or to place a dish where they give a trencher"; and speaking of the passion of people for raising themselves above their extraction, the writer, a little farther on, observes: "For the yeoman's son, as I said before, leaving gee haigh! for, Butler, some more fair trenchers to the table! bringeth these ensuing ulcers amongst the members of the common body."

The employment of trenchers, which originated in the manner which I have shown, introduced the custom of the distribution at table of the two sexes, and the fashion of placing a lady and gentleman alternately. In former days it was frequently usual for a couple thus seated together to eat from one trencher, more particularly if the relations between them were of an intimate nature, or, again, if it were the master and mistress of the establishment. Walpole relates that so late as the middle of the last century the old Duke and Duchess of Hamilton occupied the dais at the head of the room, and preserved the traditional manner by sharing the same plate. It was a token of attachment and a tender recollection of unreturnable youth.

The prejudice against the fork in England remained very steadfast actual centuries after its first introduction; forks are particularised among the treasures of kings, as if they had been crown jewels, in the same manner as the *iron* spits, pots, and frying-pans of his Majesty Edward III.; and even so late as the seventeeth century, Coryat, who employed one after his visit to Italy, was nicknamed "Furcifer." The two-pronged implement long outlived Coryat; and it is to be seen in cutlers' signs even down to our day. The old dessert set, curiously enough, instead of consisting of knives and forks in equal proportions, contained eleven knives and one fork for *ginger*. Both the fork and spoon were frequently made with handles of glass or crystal, like those of mother-of-pearl at present in vogue.

In a tract coeval with Coryat the Fork-bearer, Breton's "Court and Country," 1618, there is a passage very relevant to this part of the theme:--"For us in the country," says he, "when we have washed our hands after no foul work, nor handling any unwholesome thing, we need no little forks to make hay with our mouths, to throw our meat into them."

Forks, though not employed by the community, became part of the effects of royal and great personages, and in the inventory of Charles V. of France appear the spoon, knife, and fork. In another of the Duke of Burgundy, sixty years later (1420), knives and other implements occur, but no fork. The cutlery is described here as of German make. Brathwaite, in his "Rules for the Government of the House of an Earl," probably written about 1617, mentions knives and spoons, but not forks.

As the fork grew out of the chopstick, the spoon was probably suggested by the ladle, a form of implement employed alike by the baker and the cook; for the early tool which we see in the hands of the operative in the oven more nearly resembles in the bowl a spoon than a shovel. In India nowadays they have ladles, but not spoons. The universality of broths and semi-liquid substances, as well as the commencement of a taste for learned gravies, prompted a recourse to new expedients for communicating between the platter and the mouth; and some person of genius saw how the difficulty might be solved by adapting the ladle to individual service.

But every religion has its quota of dissent, and there were, nay, are still, many who professed adherence to the sturdy simplicity of their progenitors, and saw in this daring reform and the fallow blade of the knife a certain effeminate prodigality.

It is significant of the drift of recent years toward the monograph, that, in 1846, Mr. Westman published "The Spoon: Primitive, Egyptian, Roman, Mediaeval and Modern," with one hundred illustrations, in an octavo volume.

The luxury of carving-knives was, even in the closing years of the fifteenth century, reserved for royalty and nobility; for in the "Privy Purse Expenses of Henry VII.," under 1497, a pair is said to have cost L1 6s. 8d. of money of that day. Nothing is said of forks. But in the same account, under February 1st, 1500-1, one Mistress Brent receives 12s. (and a book, which cost the king 5s. more) for a silver fork weighing three ounces. In Newbery's "Dives Pragmaticus," 1563, a unique poetical volume in the library at Althorpe, there is a catalogue of cooking utensils which, considering its completeness, is worth quotation; the author speaks in the character of a chapman--one forestalling Autolycus:--

> "I have basins, ewers, of tin, pewter and glass.
> Great vessels of copper, fine latten and brass:
> Both pots, pans and kettles, such as never was.
> I have platters, dishes, saucers and candle-sticks,
> Chafers, lavers, towels and fine tricks:
> Posnets, frying-pans, and fine puddingpricks ...
> Fine pans for milk, and trim tubs for sowse.
> I have ladles, scummers, andirons and spits,
> Dripping-pans, pot-hooks....
> I have fire-pans, fire-forks, tongs, trivets, and trammels,
> Roast-irons, trays, flaskets, mortars and pestles...."

And among other items he adds rollers for paste, moulds for cooks, fine cutting knives, fine wine glasses, soap, fine salt, and candles. The list is the next best thing to an auctioneer's inventory of an Elizabethan kitchen, to the fittings of Shakespeare's, or rather of his father's. A good idea of the character and resources of a nobleman's or wealthy gentleman's kitchen at the end of the sixteenth and commencement of the seventeenth century may be formed from the Fairfax inventories (1594-1624), lately edited by Mr. Peacock. I propose to annex a catalogue of the utensils which there present themselves:--

The furnace pan for beef.
The beef kettle.
Great and small kettles.
Brass kettles, holding from sixteen to twenty gallons each.
Little kettles with bowed or carved handles.
Copper pans with ears.
Great brass pots.
Dripping-pans.
An iron peel or baking shovel.
A brazen mortar and a pestle.
Gridirons.
Iron ladles.
A laten scummer.
A grater.
A pepper mill.
A mustard-quern.
Boards.
A salt-box.
An iron range.
Iron racks.
A tin pot.
Pot hooks.
A galley bawk to suspend the kettle or pot over the fire.
Spits, square and round, and various sizes.
Bearers.
Crooks.

In the larders (wet and dry) and pastry were:--

Moulding boards for pastry.
A boulting tub for meal.
A little table.
A spice cupboard.
A chest for oatmeal.
A trough.
Hanging and other shelves.

Here follows the return of pewter, brass, and other vessels belonging to the kitchen:--

Pewter dishes of nine sizes (from Newcastle).
Long dishes for rabbits. }
Saucers.   }
Chargers.   } Silver fashioned.
Pie plates.   }
Voider.   }
A beef-prick.
Fire shoves and tongs.
A brig (a sort of brandreth).
A cullender.
A pewter baking-pan.
Kettles of brass.
A skillet.
A brandeth.
A shredding knife.
A chopping knife.
An apple cradle.
A pair of irons to make wafers with.
A brass pot-lid.
Beef-axes and knives. }
Slaughter ropes.   } For Slaughtering.
Beef stangs.   }

In the beef-house was an assortment of tubs, casks, and hogsheads. Table knives, forks, spoons, and drinking-vessels presumably belonged to another department.

The dripping-pan is noticed in Breton's "Fantasticks," 1626: "Dishes and trenchers are necessary servants, and they that have no meat may go scrape; a Spit and a Dripping-pan would do well, if well furnished." Flecknoe, again, in his character of a "Miserable old Gentlewoman," inserted among his "Enigmatical Characters," 1658, speaks of her letting her prayer-book fall into the dripping-pan, and the dog and the cat quarrelling over it, and at last agreeing to pray on it!

But this is a branch of the subject I cannot afford further to penetrate. Yet I must say a word about the polished maple-wood bowl, or **maser**, with its mottoes and quaint devices, which figured on the side-board of the yeoman and the franklin, and which Chaucer must have often seen in their homes. Like everything else which becomes popular, it was copied in the precious metals, with costly and elaborate goldsmith's work; but its interest for us is local, and does not lend itself to change of material and neighbourhood. The habits of the poor and middle classes are apt to awaken a keener curiosity in our minds from the comparatively slender information which has come to us upon them; and as in the case of the maser, the laver which was employed in humble circles for washing the hands before and after a meal was, not of gold or silver, as in the houses of the nobility, but of brass or laten, nor was it in either instance a ceremonious form, but a necessary process. The modern finger-glass and rose-water dish, which are an incidence of every entertainment of pretension, and in higher society as much a parcel of the dinner-table as knives and forks, are, from a mediaeval standpoint, luxurious anachronisms.

In Archbishop Alfric's "Colloquy," originally written in the tenth century, and subsequently augmented and enriched with a Saxon gloss by one of his pupils, the cook is one of the persons introduced and interrogated. He is asked what his profession is worth to the community; and he replies that without him people would have to eat their greens and flesh raw; whereupon it is rejoined that they might readily dress them themselves; to which the cook can only answer, that in such case all men would be reduced to the position of servants.

The kitchen had its **chef** or master-cook (archimacherus), under-cooks, a waferer or maker of sweets, a scullion or swiller (who is otherwise described as a **quistron**), and knaves, or boys for preparing the meat; and all these had their special functions and implements.

Even in the fifteenth century the appliances for cookery were evidently far more numerous than they had been. An illustrated vocabulary portrays, among other items, the dressing-board, the dressing-knife, the roasting-iron, the frying-pan, the spit-turner (in lieu of the old turn-broach), the andiron, the ladle, the slice, the skummer; and the ***assitabulum***, or saucer, first presents itself. It seems as if the butler and the pantler had their own separate quarters; and the different species of wine, and the vessels for holding it, are not forgotten. The archaic pantry was dedicated, not to its later objects, but to that which the name strictly signifies; but at the same time the writer warrants us in concluding, that the pantry accommodated certain miscellaneous utensils, as he comprises in its contents a candlestick, a table or board-cloth, a hand-cloth or napkin, a drinking bowl, a saucer, and a spoon. The kitchen, in short, comprised within its boundaries a far larger variety of domestic requisites of all kinds than its modern representative, which deals with an external machinery so totally changed. The ancient Court of England was so differently constituted from the present, and so many offices which sprang out of the feudal system have fallen into desuetude, that it requires a considerable effort to imagine a condition of things, where the master-cook of our lord the king was a personage of high rank and extended possessions. How early the functions of cook and the property attached to the position were separated, and the tenure of the land made dependent on a nominal ceremony, is not quite clear. Warner thinks that it was in the Conqueror's time; but at any rate, in that of Henry II. the husband of the heiress of Bartholomew de Cheney held his land in Addington, Surrey, by the serjeantry of finding a cook to dress the victuals at the coronation; the custom was kept up at least so late as the reign of George III., to whom at his coronation the lord of the manor of Addington presented a dish of pottage. The tenure was varied in its details from time to time. But for my purpose it is sufficient that manorial rights were acquired by the magnus coquus or magister coquorum in the same way as by the grand butler and other officers of state; and when so large a share of the splendour of royalty continued for centuries to emanate from the kitchen, it was scarcely inappropriate or unfair to confer on that department of state some titular distinction, and endow the holder with substantial honours. To the Grand Chamberlain and the Grand Butler the Grand Cook was a meet appendage.

The primary object of these feudal endowments was the establishment of a cordon round the throne of powerful subjects under conditions and titles which to ourselves may appear incongruous and obscure, but which were in tolerable keeping with the financial and commercial organisation of the period, with a restricted currency, a revenue chiefly payable in kind, scanty facilities for transit, and an absence of trading centres. These steward-ships, butler-ships, and cook-ships, in the hands of the most trusted vassals of the Crown, constituted a rudimentary vehicle for in-gathering the dues of all kinds renderable by the king's tenants; and as an administrative scheme gradually unfolded itself, they became titular and honorary, like our own reduced menagerie of nondescripts. But while they lasted in their substance and reality, they answered the wants and notions of a primitive people; nor is it for this practical age to lift up its hands or its voice too high; for mediaeval England is still legible without much excavation in our Court, our Church, nay, in our Laws. There lurk our cunning spoilers!

Mr. Fairholt, in the "Archaeological Album," 1845, has depicted for our benefit the *chef* of the Abbey of St. Albans in the fourteenth century, and his wife Helena The representations of these two notable personages occur in a MS. in the British Museum, which formerly belonged to the Abbey, and contains a list of its benefactors, with their gifts. It does not appear that Master Robert, cook to Abbot Thomas, was the donor of any land or money; but, in consideration of his long and faithful services, his soul was to be prayed for with that of his widow, who bestowed 3s. 4d. ad opus hujus libri, which Fairholt supposes to refer to the insertion of her portrait and that of her spouse among the graphic decorations of the volume. They are perhaps in their way unique. Behold them opposite!

Another point in reference to the early economy of the table, which should not be overlooked, is the character of the ancient buttery, and the quick transition which its functionary, the butler, experienced from the performance of special to that of general duties.

He at a very remote period acted not merely as the curator of the wine-cellar, but as the domestic steward and storekeeper; and it was his business to provide for the requirements of the kitchen and the pantry, and to see that no opportunity was neglected of supplying, from the nearest port, or market town, or fair, if his employer resided in the country, all the necessaries for the departments under his control. We are apt to regard the modern bearer of the same title as more catholic in his employments than the appellation suggests; but he in fact wields, on the contrary, a very circumscribed authority compared to that of his feudal prototype.

One of the menial offices in the kitchen, when the spit came into use, was the broach-turner, lately referred to. He was by no means invariably maintained on the staff, but was hired for the occasion, which may augur the general preference for boiled and fried meats. Sometimes it appears that any lad passing by, or in want of temporary employment, was admitted for this purpose, and had a trifling gratuity, or perhaps only his dinner and the privilege of dipping his fingers in the dripping, for his pains.

Warner cites an entry in some accounts of the Hospital of St. Bartholomew at Sandwich, under 1569:--"For tournynge the spytte, iiijd." and this was when the mayor of the borough dined with the prior. A royal personage gave, of course, more. The play of "Gammer Gurton's Needle," written about 1560, opens with a speech of Diccon the Bedlam, or poor Tom, where he says:--

"Many a gossip's cup in my time have I tasted,
  And many a broach and spit have I both turned and basted."

The spit, again, was supplanted by the jack.

The "History of Friar Rush," 1620, opens with a scene in which the hero introduces himself to a monastery, and is sent by the unsuspecting prior to the master-cook, who finds him subordinate employment.

MEALS.

It has been noted that for a great length of time two meals were made to suffice the requirements of all classes. Our own experience shows how immaterial the names are which people from age to age choose to bestow on their feeding intervals. Some call supper *dinner*, and others call dinner *luncheon.* First comes the prevailing mode instituted by fashionable society, and then a foolish subscription to it by a section of the community who are too poor to follow it, and too proud not to seem to do so. Formerly it was usual for the Great to dine and sup earlier than the Little; but now the rule is reversed, and the later a man dines the more distinguished he argues himself. We have multiplied our daily seasons of refreshment, and eat and drink far oftener than our ancestors; but the truly genteel Briton never sups; the word is scarcely in his vocabulary,--like Beau Brummel and the farthing--"Fellow, I do not know the coin!"

In a glossary of the tenth-eleventh century only two meals are quoted: under-meat = ***prandium***, and even-meat = ***coena***. That is to say, our Saxon precursors were satisfied as a rule with two repasts daily, but to this in more luxurious times were added the supper and even the rear-supper, the latter being, so far as we know, a second course or dessert and the bipartite collation corresponding to the modern late dinner. But it is one of those strange survivals of ancient manners which people practise without any consciousness of the fact, which is at the root of the fashion, which still occasionally prevails, of dividing the chief meal of the day by an interval of repose, and taking the wine and dessert an hour or two after the other courses; and the usage in our colleges and inns of court of retiring to another apartment to "wine" may claim the same origin. It is obvious that the rear-supper was susceptible of becoming the most important and costly part of an entertainment; and that it frequently assumed extravagant proportions, many passages from our early poets might be adduced to prove.

In the "Book of Cookery," 1500, we have the ***menu*** at the installation of Arch-bishop Nevill in York in 1467; but the bill of fare of a feast given by him in 1452 at Oxford, where he is mentioned as Master Nevill, son of the Earl of Salisbury, is inserted from the Cotton MS. Titus, in "Reliquiae Antiquae," 1841. It consisted of three courses, which seem to have been the customary limit. Of course, however, the usage varied, as in the "Song of the Boar's Head," of which there are two or three versions, two courses only are specified in what has the air of having been a rather sumptuous entertainment.

The old low-Latin term for the noonday meal was ***merenda***, which suggests the idea of food to be earned before it was enjoyed. So in "Friar Bacon's Prophesie," 1604, a poem, it is declared that, in the good old days, he that wrought not, till he sweated, was held unworthy of his meat. This reminds one of Abernethy's maxim for the preservation of health,--to live on sixpence a day, and earn it.

The "Song of the Boar's Head," just cited, and printed from the Porkington MS. in "Reliquiae Antiquae" (ii, 30), refers to larks for ladies to pick as part of the second course in a banquet. On special occasions, in the middle ages, after the dessert, hippocras was served, as they have liqueurs to this day on the Continent both after dinner and after the mid-day breakfast.

The writer of "Piers of Fulham" lived to see this fashion of introducing a third meal, and that again split into two for luxury's sake; for his metrical biographer tells us, that he refused rear-suppers, from a fear of surfeiting.

I collect that in the time of Henry VIII. the supper was a well-established institution, and that the abuse of postponing it to a too advanced hour had crept in; for the writer of a poem of this period especially counsels his readers not to sup late.

Rear-suppers were not only held in private establishments, but in taverns; and in the early interlude of the "Four Elements," given in my edition of Dodsley, and originally published about 1519, a very graphic and edifying scene occurs of a party of roisterers ordering and enjoying an entertainment of this kind. About seventy years later, Robert Greene, the playwright, fell a victim to a surfeit of pickled herrings and Rhenish wine, at some merry gathering of his intimates falling under this denomination. Who will venture to deny that the first person who kept unreasonable hours was an author and a poet? Even Shakespeare is not exempt from the suspicion of having hastened his end by indulgence with one or two friends in a gay carouse of this kind.

The author of the "Description of England" enlightens us somewhat on the sort of kitchen which the middle class and yeomanry of his time deemed fit and sufficient. The merchant or private gentleman had usually from one to three dishes on the table when there were no visitors, and from four to six when there was company. What the yeoman's every-day diet was Harrison does not express; but at Christmas he had brawn, pudding and souse, with mustard; beef, mutton, and pork; shred pies, goose, pig, capon, turkey, veal, cheese, apples, etc., with good drink, and a blazing fire in the hall. The farmer's bill of fare varied according to the season: in Lent, red herrings and salt fish; at Easter, veal and bacon; at Martinmas, salted beef; at Midsummer, fresh beef, peas, and salad; at Michaelmas, fresh herrings and fat mutton; at All Saints', pork and peas and fish; and at Christmas, the same dainties as our yeoman, with good cheer and pastime.

The modern luncheon or nuncheon was the archaic *prandium*, or under-meat, displaced by the breakfast, and modified in its character by the different distribution of the daily repasts, so that, instead of being the earliest regular meal, like the grand dejeuner of the French, or coming, like our luncheon, between breakfast and dinner, it interposed itself between the noontide dinner and the evening supper. Now, with an increasing proportion of the community, the universal luncheon, postponed to a later hour, is the actual dinner; and our under-meal is the afternoon tea.

In those not-wholly-to-be-discommended days, the residue of the meal was consumed in the servants' hall, and the scraps bestowed on the poor at the gate; and the last part of the business was carried out, not as a matter of chance or caprice, but on as methodical a principle as the payment of a poor-rate. At the servants' table, besides the waiters and other attendants on the principal board, mentioned by Harrison, sat the master-cook, the pantler, the steward or major-domo, the butler, the cellarman, the waferer, and others. It was not till comparatively recent times that the *wafery*, a special department of the royal kitchen, where the confectionery and pastry were prepared, was discontinued.

There was necessarily a very large section of the community in all the large towns, especially in London, which was destitute of culinary appliances, and at the same time of any charitable or eleemosynary privileges. A multitude of persons, of both sexes and all ages, gradually developed itself, having no feudal ties, but attached to an endless variety of more or less humble employments.

How did all these men, women, boys, girls, get their daily food? The answer is, in the public eating-houses. Fitzstephen tells us that in the reign of Henry II. (1154-89), besides the wine-vaults and the shops which sold liquors, there was on the banks of the river a public eating-house or cook's-shop, where, according to the time of year, you could get every kind of victuals, roasted, boiled, baked, or fried; and even, says he, if a friend should arrive at a citizen's house, and not care to wait, they go to the shop, where there were viands always kept ready to suit every purse and palate, even including venison, sturgeon, and Guinea-fowls. For all classes frequented the City; and before Bardolph's day noblemen and gentlemen came to Smithfield to buy their horses, as they did to the waterside near the Tower to embark for a voyage.

One of the characters in the "Canterbury Tales"--the Cook of London--was, in fact the keeper of a cook's-shop; and in the Prologue to the Tale, with which his name is associated, the charming story of "Gamelin," the poet makes the Reeve charge his companion with not very creditable behaviour towards his customers. So our host trusts that his relation will be entertaining and good:--

"For many a pasty hast thou let blood,
    And many a Jack of Dover[13] hast thou sold, That
hath been twice hot and twice cold.
    Of many a pilgrim hast thou Christ's curse--
    For thy parsley fare they yet the worse:
    That they have eaten with the stubble goose,
    For in thy shop is many a fly loose."

But these restaurants were not long confined to one locality. From a very early date, owing perhaps to its proximity to the Tower and the Thames, East Cheap was famed for its houses of entertainment. The Dagger in Cheap is mentioned in "A Hundred Merry Tales," 1526. The Boar is historical. It was naturally at the East-end, in London proper, that the flood-tide, as it were, of tavern life set in, among the seafarers, in the heart of industrial activity; and the anecdotes and glimpses which we enjoy show, just what might have been guessed, that these houses often became scenes of riotous excess and debauch. Lydgate's ballad of "London Lickpenny" helps one to imagine what such resorts must have been in the first part of the fifteenth century. It is almost permissible to infer that the street contained, in addition to the regular inns, an assortment of open counters, where the commodities on sale were cried aloud for the benefit of the passer-by; for he says:--

"When I hied me into East Cheap:
    One cries ribs of beef, and many a pie:
    Pewter pots they clattered on a heap;
There was harp, fife, and sautry."

---

13 A sole

The mention of pewter is noteworthy, because the Earl of Northumberland ate his dinner off wood in 1572. Pewter plates had not long been given up when I joined the Inner Temple in 1861.

There is a still more interesting allusion in the interlude of the "World and the Child," 1522, where Folly is made to say:--

> "Yea, and we shall be right welcome, I dare well say,
>   In East Cheap for to dine;
>   And then we will with Lombards at passage play,
>   And at the Pope's Head sweet wine assay."

The places of resort in this rollicking locality could furnish, long before The Boar made the acquaintance of Falstaff, every species of delicacy and bonne bouche to their constituents, and the revelry was apt sometimes to extend to an unseasonable hour. In an early naval song we meet with the lines:

> "He that will in East Cheap eat a goose so fat,
>   With harp, pipe, and song,
>   Must lie in Newgate on a mat,
>   Be the night never so long."

And these establishments infallibly contributed their quota or more to the prisons in the vicinity.

Houses of refreshment seem, however, to have extended themselves westward, and to have become tolerably numerous, in the earlier society of the sixteenth century, for Sir Thomas More, in a letter to his friend Dean Colet, speaking of a late walk in Westminster and of the various temptations to expenditure and dissipation which the neighbourhood then afforded, remarks: "Whithersoever we cast our eyes, what do we see but victualling-houses, fishmongers, butchers, cooks, pudding-makers, fishers, and fowlers, who minister matter to our bellies?" This was prior to 1519, the date of Colet's decease.

There were of course periods of scarcity and high prices then as now. It was only a few years later (1524), that Robert Whittinton, in one of his grammatical tracts (the "Vulgaria"), includes among his examples:--

"Befe and motton is so dere, that a peny worth of meet wyll scant suffyse a boy at a meale."

The term "cook's-shop" occurs in the Orders and Ordinances devised by the Steward, Dean, and Burgesses of Westminster in 1585, for the better municipal government of that borough.

The tenth article runs thus:--"Item, that no person or persons that keepeth or that hereafter shall keep any cook's-shop, shall also keep a common ale-house (except every such person shall be lawfully licensed thereunto), upon pain to have and receive such punishment, and pay such fine, as by the statute in that case is made and provided."

But while the keepers of restaurants were, as a rule, precluded by law from selling ale, the publicans on their side were not supposed to purvey refreshment other than their own special commodities. For the fifteenth proviso of these orders is:--

"Item, that no tavern-keeper or inn-keeper shall keep any cook shop upon pain to forfeit and pay for every time offending therein 4d."

The London cooks became famous, and were not only in demand in the City and its immediate outskirts, but were put into requisition when any grand entertainment was given in the country. In the list of expenses incurred at the reception of Queen Elizabeth in 1577 by Lord Keeper Bacon at Gorhambury, is an item of L12 as wages to the cooks of London. An accredited anecdote makes Bacon's father inimical to too lavish an outlay in the kitchen; but a far more profuse housekeeper might have been puzzled to dispense with special help, where the consumption of viands and the consequent culinary labour and skill required, were so unusually great.

In the Prologue to the "Canterbury Tales," the Cook of London and his qualifications are thus emblazoned:--

"A Cook thei hadde with hem for the nones,
    To boylle chyknes, with the mary

bones,   And poudre marchaunt tart, and galyngale;
    Wel cowde he knowe a draugte of London ale.

He cowde roste, and sethe, and broille, and frie
Maken mortreux, and wel bake a pie.
But gret harm was it, as it thoughte me,
That on his schyne a mormal had he:
For blankmanger that made he with the beste."

This description would be hardly worth quoting, if it were not for the source whence it comes, and the names which it presents in common with the "Form of Cury" and other ancient relics. Chaucer's Cook was a personage of unusually wide experience, having, in his capacity as the keeper of an eating-house, to cater for so many customers of varying tastes and resources.

In the time of Elizabeth, the price at an ordinary for a dinner seems to have been sixpence. It subsequently rose to eightpence; and in the time of George I. the "Vade Mecum for Malt Worms (1720)" speaks of the landlord of The Bell, in Carter Lane, raising his tariff to tenpence. In comparison with the cost of a similar meal at present, all these quotations strike one as high, when the different value of money is considered. But in 1720, at all events, the customer ate at his own discretion.

Their vicinity to East Cheap, the great centre of early taverns and cook's-shops, obtained for Pudding Lane and Pie Corner those savoury designations.

Paris, like London, had its cook's-shops, where you might eat your dinner on the premises, or have it brought to your lodging in a covered dish by a ***porte-chape.*** In the old prints of French kitchen interiors, the cook's inseparable companion is his ladle, which he used for stirring and serving, and occasionally for dealing a refractory garcon de cuisine a rap on the head.

The Dictionary of Johannes de Garlandia (early thirteenth century) represents the cooks at Paris as imposing on the ignorant and inexperienced badly cooked or even tainted meat, which injured their health. These "coquinarii" stood, perhaps, in the same relation to those times as our keepers of restaurants.

He mentions in another place that the cooks washed their utensils in hot water, as well as the plates and dishes on which the victuals were served.

Mr. Wright has cited an instance from the romance of "Doon de Mayence," where the guards of a castle, on a warm summer evening, partook of their meal in a field. Refreshment in the open air was also usual in the hunting season, when a party were at a distance from home; and the garden arbour was occasionally converted to this kind of purpose, when it had assumed its more modern phase. But our picnic was unknown.

ETIQUETTE OF THE TABLE.

Paul Hentzner, who was in England at the end of the reign of Elizabeth, remarks of the people whom he saw that "they are more polite in eating than the French, devouring less bread, but more meat, which they roast in perfection. They put a good deal of sugar in their drink."

In his "Court and Country," 1618, Nicholas Breton gives an instructive account of the strict rules which were drawn up for observance in great households at that time, and says that the gentlemen who attended on great lords and ladies had enough to do to carry these orders out. Not a trencher must be laid or a napkin folded awry; not a dish misplaced; not a capon carved or a rabbit unlaced contrary to the usual practice; not a glass filled or a cup uncovered save at the appointed moment: everybody must stand, speak, and look according to regulation.

The books of demeanour which have been collected by Mr. Furnivall for the Early English Text Society have their incidental value as illustrating the immediate theme, and are curious, from the growth in consecutive compilations of the code of instructions for behaviour at table, as evidences of an increasing cultivation both in manners and the variety of appliances for domestic use, including relays of knives for the successive courses. Distinctions were gradually drawn between genteel and vulgar or coarse ways of eating, and facilities were provided for keeping the food from direct contact with the fingers, and other primitive offences against decorum. Many of the precepts in the late fifteenth century "Babies' Book," while they demonstrate the necessity for admonition, speak also to an advance in politeness and delicacy at table. There must be a beginning somewhere; and the authors of these guides to deportment had imbibed the feeling for something higher and better, before they undertook to communicate their views to the young generation.

There is no doubt that the "Babies' Book" and its existing congeners are the successors of anterior and still more imperfect attempts to introduce at table some degree of cleanliness and decency. When the "Babies' Book" made its appearance, the progress in this direction must have been immense. But the observance of such niceties was of course at first exceptional; and the ideas which we see here embodied were very sparingly carried into practice outside the verge of the Court itself and the homes of a few of the aristocracy.

There may be an inclination to revolt against the barbarous doggerel in which the instruction is, as a rule, conveyed, and against the tedious process of perusing a series of productions which follow mainly the same lines. But it is to be recollected that these manuals were necessarily renewed in the manuscript form from age to age, with variations and additions, and that the writers resorted to metre as a means of impressing the rules of conduct more forcibly on their pupils.

Of all the works devoted to the management of the table and kitchen, the "Book of Nurture," by John Russell, usher of the chamber and marshal of the ball to Humphrey, Duke of Gloucester, is perhaps, on the whole, the most elaborate, most trustworthy, and most important. It leaves little connected with the *cuisine* of a noble establishment of the fifteenth century untouched and unexplained; and although it assumes the metrical form, and in a literary respect is a dreary performance, its value as a guide to almost every branch of the subject is indubitable. It lays bare to our eyes the entire machinery of the household, and we gain a clearer insight from it than from the rest of the group of treatises, not merely into what a great man of those days and his family and retainers ate and drank, and how they used to behave themselves at table, but into the process of making various drinks, the mystery of carving, and the division of duties among the members of the staff. It is, in fact, the earliest comprehensive book in our literature.

The functions of the squire at the table of a prince are, to a certain extent, shown in the "Squire of Low Degree," where the hero, having arrayed himself in scarlet, with a chaplet on his head and a belt round his waist, cast a horn about his neck, and went to perform his duty in the hall. He approaches the king, dish in hand, and kneels. When he has served his sovereign, he hands the meats to the others. We see a handsome assortment of victuals on this occasion, chiefly venison and birds, and some of the latter were baked in bread, probably a sort of paste. The majority of the names on the list are familiar, but a few--the teal, the curlew, the crane, the stork, and the snipe--appear to be new. It is, in all these cases, almost impossible to be sure how much we owe to the poet's imagination and how much to his rhythmical poverty. From another passage it is to be inferred that baked venison was a favourite mode of dressing the deer.

The precaution of coming to table with clean hands was inculcated perhaps first as a necessity, when neither forks nor knives were used, and subsequently as a mark of breeding. The knife preceded the spoon, and the fork, which had been introduced into Italy in the eleventh century, and which strikes one as a fortuitous development of the Oriental chopstick, came last. It was not in general use even in the seventeenth century here. Coryat the traveller saw it among the Italians, and deemed it a luxury and a notable fact.

The precepts delivered by Lydgate and others for demeanour at table were in advance of the age, and were probably as much honoured in the breach as otherwise. But the common folk did then much as many of them do now, and granted themselves a dispensation both from knife and fork, and soap and water. The country boor still eats his bacon or his herring with his fingers, just as Charles XII. of Sweden buttered his bread with his royal thumb.

A certain cleanliness of person, which, at the outset, was not considerably regarded, became customary, as manners softened and female influence asserted itself; and even Lydgate, in his "Stans Puer ad Mensam (an adaptation from Sulpitius)," enjoins on his page or serving-boy a resort to the lavatory before he proceeds to discharge his functions at the board--

> "Pare clean thy nails; thy hands wash also
>   Before meat; and when thou dost arise."

Other precepts follow. He was not to speak with his mouth full. He was to wipe his lips after eating, and his spoon when he had finished, taking care not to leave it in his dish. He was to keep his napkin as clean and neat as possible, and he was not to pick his teeth with his knife. He was not to put too much on his trencher at once. He was not to drop his sauce or soup over his clothes, or to fill his spoon too full, or to bring dirty knives to the table. All these points of conduct are graphic enough; and their trite character is their virtue.

Boiled, and perhaps fried meats were served on silver; but roasts might be brought to table on the spit, which, after a while, was often of silver, and handed round for each person to cut what he pleased; and this was done not only with ordinary meat, but with game, and even with a delicacy like a roast peacock. Of smaller birds, several were broached on one spit. There is a mediaeval story of a husband being asked by his wife to help her to the several parts of a fowl in succession, till nothing was left but the implement on which it had come in, whereupon the man determined she should have that too, and belaboured her soundly with it. At more ceremonious banquets the servants were preceded by music, or their approach from the kitchen to the hall was proclaimed by sound of trumpets. Costly plate was gradually introduced, as well as linen and utensils, for the table; but the plate may be conjectured to have been an outcome from the primitive **trencher**, a large slice of bread on which meat was laid for the occupants of the high table, and which was cast aside after use.

Bread served at table was not to be bitten or broken off the loaf, but to be cut; and the loaf was sometimes divided before the meal, and skilfully pieced together again, so as to be ready for use.

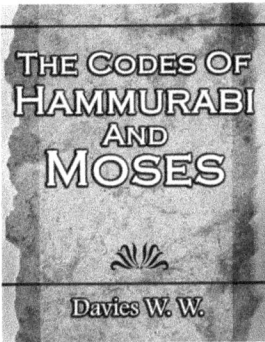

The Codes Of Hammurabi And Moses
W. W. Davies

QTY

The discovery of the Hammurabi Code is one of the greatest achievements of archaeology, and is of paramount interest, not only to the student of the Bible, but also to all those interested in ancient history...

Religion   **ISBN: *1-59462-338-4***   Pages:132
MSRP $12.95

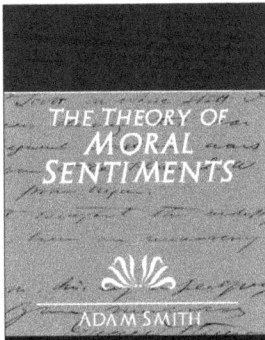

The Theory of Moral Sentiments
Adam Smith

QTY

This work from 1749. contains original theories of conscience amd moral judgment and it is the foundation for systemof morals.

Philosophy   **ISBN: *1-59462-777-0***   Pages:536
MSRP $19.95

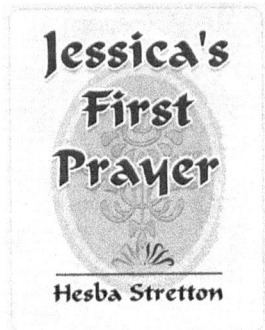

Jessica's First Prayer
Hesba Stretton

QTY

In a screened and secluded corner of one of the many railway-bridges which span the streets of London there could be seen a few years ago, from five o'clock every morning until half past eight, a tidily set-out coffee-stall, consisting of a trestle and board, upon which stood two large tin cans, with a small fire of charcoal burning under each so as to keep the coffee boiling during the early hours of the morning when the work-people were thronging into the city on their way to their daily toil...

Childrens   **ISBN: *1-59462-373-2***   Pages:84
MSRP $9.95

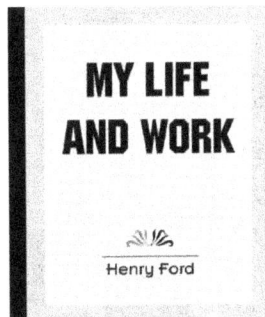

My Life and Work
Henry Ford

QTY

Henry Ford revolutionized the world with his implementation of mass production for the Model T automobile. Gain valuable business insight into his life and work with his own auto-biography... "We have only started on our development of our country we have not as yet, with all our talk of wonderful progress, done more than scratch the surface. The progress has been wonderful enough but..."

Biographies/   **ISBN: *1-59462-198-5***   Pages:300
MSRP $21.95

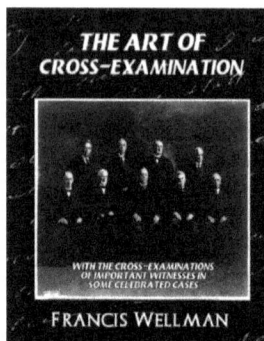

The Art of Cross-Examination
Francis Wellman

QTY

I presume it is the experience of every author, after his first book is published upon an important subject, to be almost overwhelmed with a wealth of ideas and illustrations which could readily have been included in his book, and which to his own mind, at least, seem to make a second edition inevitable. Such certainly was the case with me; and when the first edition had reached its sixth impression in five months, I rejoiced to learn that it seemed to my publishers that the book had met with a sufficiently favorable reception to justify a second and considerably enlarged edition. ..

Pages:412

Reference   ISBN: *1-59462-647-2*   *MSRP $19.95*

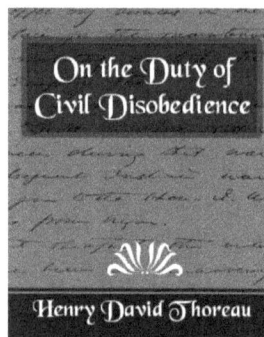

On the Duty of Civil Disobedience
Henry David Thoreau

QTY

Thoreau wrote his famous essay, On the Duty of Civil Disobedience, as a protest against an unjust but popular war and the immoral but popular institution of slave-owning. He did more than write—he declined to pay his taxes, and was hauled off to gaol in consequence. Who can say how much this refusal of his hastened the end of the war and of slavery ?

Law   ISBN: *1-59462-747-9*   **Pages:48**

MSRP $7.45

Dream Psychology Psychoanalysis for Beginners
Sigmund Freud

QTY

Sigmund Freud, born Sigismund Schlomo Freud (May 6, 1856 - September 23, 1939), was a Jewish-Austrian neurologist and psychiatrist who co-founded the psychoanalytic school of psychology. Freud is best known for his theories of the unconscious mind, especially involving the mechanism of repression; his redefinition of sexual desire as mobile and directed towards a wide variety of objects; and his therapeutic techniques, especially his understanding of transference in the therapeutic relationship and the presumed value of dreams as sources of insight into unconscious desires.

Pages:196

Psychology   ISBN: *1-59462-905-6*   *MSRP $15.45*

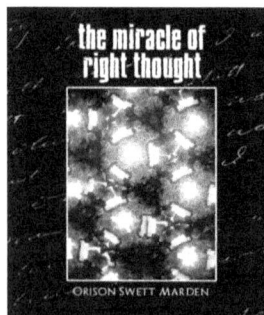

The Miracle of Right Thought
Orison Swett Marden

QTY

Believe with all of your heart that you will do what you were made to do. When the mind has once formed the habit of holding cheerful, happy, prosperous pictures, it will not be easy to form the opposite habit. It does not matter how improbable or how far away this realization may see, or how dark the prospects may be, if we visualize them as best we can, as vividly as possible, hold tenaciously to them and vigorously struggle to attain them, they will gradually become actualized, realized in the life. But a desire, a longing without endeavor, a yearning abandoned or held indifferently will vanish without realization.

Pages:360

Self Help   ISBN: *1-59462-644-8*   *MSRP $25.45*

QTY

The Rosicrucian Cosmo-Conception Mystic Christianity by *Max Heindel*   ISBN: *1-59462-188-8* **$38.95**
The Rosicrucian Cosmo-conception is not dogmatic, neither does it appeal to any other authority than the reason of the student. It is: not controversial, but is: sent forth in the, hope that it may help to clear...   New Age/Religion Pages 646

Abandonment To Divine Providence by *Jean-Pierre de Caussade*   ISBN: *1-59462-228-0* **$25.95**
"The Rev. Jean Pierre de Caussade was one of the most remarkable spiritual writers of the Society of Jesus in France in the 18th Century. His death took place at Toulouse in 1751. His works have gone through many editions and have been republished...   Inspirational/Religion Pages 400

Mental Chemistry by *Charles Haanel*   ISBN: *1-59462-192-6* **$23.95**
Mental Chemistry allows the change of material conditions by combining and appropriately utilizing the power of the mind. Much like applied chemistry creates something new and unique out of careful combinations of chemicals the mastery of mental chemistry...   New Age Pages 354

The Letters of Robert Browning and Elizabeth Barret Barrett 1845-1846 vol II   ISBN: *1-59462-193-4* **$35.95**
by *Robert Browning* and *Elizabeth Barrett*   Biographies Pages 596

Gleanings In Genesis (volume I) by *Arthur W. Pink*   ISBN: *1-59462-130-6* **$27.45**
Appropriately has Genesis been termed "the seed plot of the Bible" for in it we have, in germ form, almost all of the great doctrines which are afterwards fully developed in the books of Scripture which follow...   Religion/Inspirational Pages 420

The Master Key by *L. W. de Laurence*   ISBN: *1-59462-001-6* **$30.95**
In no branch of human knowledge has there been a more lively increase of the spirit of research during the past few years than in the study of Psychology, Concentration and Mental Discipline. The requests for authentic lessons in Thought Control, Mental Discipline and...   New Age/Business Pages 422

The Lesser Key Of Solomon Goetia by *L. W. de Laurence*   ISBN: *1-59462-092-X* **$9.95**
This translation of the first book of the "Lernegton" which is now for the first time made accessible to students of Talismanic Magic was done, after careful collation and edition, from numerous Ancient Manuscripts in Hebrew, Latin, and French...   New Age/Occult Pages 92

Rubaiyat Of Omar Khayyam by *Edward Fitzgerald*   ISBN:*1-59462-332-5* **$13.95**
Edward Fitzgerald, whom the world has already learned, in spite of his own efforts to remain within the shadow of anonymity, to look upon as one of the rarest poets of the century, was born at Bredfield, in Suffolk, on the 31st of March, 1809. He was the third son of John Purcell...   Music Pages 172

Ancient Law by *Henry Maine*   ISBN: *1-59462-128-4* **$29.95**
The chief object of the following pages is to indicate some of the earliest ideas of mankind, as they are reflected in Ancient Law, and to point out the relation of those ideas to modern thought.   Religion/History Pages 452

Far-Away Stories by *William J. Locke*   ISBN: *1-59462-129-2* **$19.45**
"Good wine needs no bush, but a collection of mixed vintages does. And this book is just such a collection. Some of the stories I do not want to remain buried for ever in the museum files of dead magazine-numbers an author's not unpardonable vanity..."   Fiction Pages 272

Life of David Crockett by *David Crockett*   ISBN: *1-59462-250-7* **$27.45**
"Colonel David Crockett was one of the most remarkable men of the times in which he lived. Born in humble life, but gifted with a strong will, an indomitable courage, and unremitting perseverance...   Biographies/New Age Pages 424

Lip-Reading by *Edward Nitchie*   ISBN: *1-59462-206-X* **$25.95**
Edward B. Nitchie, founder of the New York School for the Hard of Hearing, now the Nitchie School of Lip-Reading, Inc, wrote "LIP-READING Principles and Practice". The development and perfecting of this meritorious work on lip-reading was an undertaking...   How-to Pages 400

A Handbook of Suggestive Therapeutics, Applied Hypnotism, Psychic Science   ISBN: *1-59462-214-0* **$24.95**
by *Henry Munro*   Health/New Age/Health/Self-help Pages 376

A Doll's House: and Two Other Plays by *Henrik Ibsen*   ISBN: *1-59462-112-8* **$19.95**
Henrik Ibsen created this classic when in revolutionary 1848 Rome. Introducing some striking concepts in playwriting for the realist genre, this play has been studied the world over.   Fiction/Classics/Plays 308

The Light of Asia by *sir Edwin Arnold*   ISBN: *1-59462-204-3* **$13.95**
In this poetic masterpiece, Edwin Arnold describes the life and teachings of Buddha. The man who was to become known as Buddha to the world was born as Prince Gautama of India but he rejected the worldly riches and abandoned the reigns of power when...   Religion/History/Biographies Pages 170

The Complete Works of Guy de Maupassant by *Guy de Maupassant*   ISBN: *1-59462-157-8* **$16.95**
"For days and days, nights and nights, I had dreamed of that first kiss which was to consecrate our engagement, and I knew not on what spot I should put my lips..."   Fiction/Classics Pages 240

The Art of Cross-Examination by *Francis L. Wellman*   ISBN: *1-59462-309-0* **$26.95**
Written by a renowned trial lawyer, Wellman imparts his experience and uses case studies to explain how to use psychology to extract desired information through questioning.   How-to/Science/Reference Pages 408

Answered or Unanswered? by *Louisa Vaughan*   ISBN: *1-59462-248-5* **$10.95**
Miracles of Faith in China   Religion Pages 112

The Edinburgh Lectures on Mental Science (1909) by *Thomas*   ISBN: *1-59462-008-3* **$11.95**
This book contains the substance of a course of lectures recently given by the writer in the Queen Street Hail, Edinburgh. Its purpose is to indicate the Natural Principles governing the relation between Mental Action and Material Conditions...   New Age/Psychology Pages 148

Ayesha by *H. Rider Haggard*   ISBN: *1-59462-301-5* **$24.95**
Verily and indeed it is the unexpected that happens! Probably if there was one person upon the earth from whom the Editor of this, and of a certain previous history, did not expect to hear again...   Classics Pages 380

Ayala's Angel by *Anthony Trollope*   ISBN: *1-59462-352-X* **$29.95**
The two girls were both pretty, but Lucy who was twenty-one who supposed to be simple and comparatively unattractive, whereas Ayala was credited, as her Bombwhat romantic name might show, with poetic charm and a taste for romance. Ayala when her father died was nineteen...   Fiction Pages 484

The American Commonwealth by *James Bryce*   ISBN: *1-59462-286-8* **$34.45**
An interpretation of American democratic political theory. It examines political mechanics and society from the perspective of Scotsman James Bryce   Politics Pages 572

Stories of the Pilgrims by *Margaret P. Pumphrey*   ISBN: *1-59462-116-0* **$17.95**
This book explores pilgrims religious oppression in England as well as their escape to Holland and eventual crossing to America on the Mayflower, and their early days in New England...   History Pages 268

QTY

The Fasting Cure *by Sinclair Upton*   ISBN: *1-59462-222-1*   **$13.95**
In the Cosmopolitan Magazine for May, 1910, and in the Contemporary Review (London) for April, 1910, I published an article dealing with my experiences in fasting. I have written a great many magazine articles, but never one which attracted so much attention...   New Age/Self Help/Health Pages 164

Hebrew Astrology *by Sepharial*   ISBN: *1-59462-308-2*   **$13.45**
In these days of advanced thinking it is a matter of common observation that we have left many of the old landmarks behind and that we are now pressing forward to greater heights and to a wider horizon than that which represented the mind-content of our progenitors...   Astrology Pages 144

Thought Vibration or The Law of Attraction in the Thought World   ISBN: *1-59462-127-6*   **$12.95**
by William Walker Atkinson   Psychology/Religion Pages 144

Optimism *by Helen Keller*   ISBN: *1-59462-108-X*   **$15.95**
Helen Keller was blind, deaf, and mute since 19 months old, yet famously learned how to overcome these handicaps, communicate with the world, and spread her lectures promoting optimism. An inspiring read for everyone...   Biographies/Inspirational Pages 84

Sara Crewe *by Frances Burnett*   ISBN: *1-59462-360-0*   **$9.45**
In the first place, Miss Minchin lived in London. Her home was a large, dull, tall one, in a large, dull square, where all the houses were alike, and all the sparrows were alike, and where all the door-knockers made the same heavy sound...   Childrens/Classic Pages 88

The Autobiography of Benjamin Franklin *by Benjamin Franklin*   ISBN: *1-59462-135-7*   **$24.95**
The Autobiography of Benjamin Franklin has probably been more extensively read than any other American historical work, and no other book of its kind has had such ups and downs of fortune. Franklin lived for many years in England, where he was agent...   Biographies/History Pages 332

Name	
Email	
Telephone	
Address	
City, State ZIP	

☐ Credit Card   ☐ Check / Money Order

Credit Card Number	
Expiration Date	
Signature	

Please Mail to: Book Jungle
PO Box 2226
Champaign, IL 61825
or Fax to: 630-214-0564

ORDERING INFORMATION
web*: www.bookjungle.com*
email*: sales@bookjungle.com*
fax*: 630-214-0564*
mail*: Book Jungle PO Box 2226 Champaign, IL 61825*
or PayPal *to sales@bookjungle.com*

Please contact us for bulk discounts

DIRECT-ORDER TERMS

20% Discount if You Order Two or More Books
Free Domestic Shipping!
Accepted: Master Card, Visa,
Discover, American Express

www.ingramcontent.com/pod-product-compliance
Lightning Source LLC
LaVergne TN
LVHW061225060426
835509LV00012B/1429